The Judges' Charter

Protecting Peoples' Rights from Tinkering Politicians

Richard Austin

1st Edition

Copyright © 2012 Richard Austin

The Author asserts the moral right to be identified as the author of this work

All rights reserved.

Please direct enquiries to:
TheJudgesCharter@hotmail.com

No part of this publication may be reproduced, stored in a retrieval system, or transmitted, in any form or by any means, electronic, mechanical, photocopying, recording or otherwise, without the prior permission of the publishers.

ISBN 978-1478217022

Cover design by Justine Elliott
Book Layout by EBooks by Design

Dedicated to

my father, Frank, the philosopher;

my mother, Karen, the warrior;

my lady, Angela, the supporter.

Contents

FOREWORD
What's it all about? 1

INTRODUCTION
Key concepts and bad myths 13

PETITION
A letter to Their Lordships 57

AFTERWORD
A 'British' Bill of Rights? 89

TIMELINE
Human Rights: A British Tale 125

REFERENCES 145

"So far as this country is concerned, every judge, on appointment, discards all politics and all prejudices. The judges have always in the past, and I hope always will, be vigilant in guarding our freedoms. Someone must be trusted. Let it be the judges."

– Lord Denning, popular British judge, speaking in 1980

Foreword

"The controversial Human Rights Act WILL be axed, David Cameron vowed yesterday. The PM pledged to replace Labour's law with a British Bill of Rights."

- Deputy Political Editor, *The Sun*

I wish to make plain from the start: this book is not about saving the Human Rights Act, even though I support the Act and believe in its values. Rather, this book is about building a 'safety net' of basic entitlements which can never be taken away from us by any political party. I shall call this safety net ***The Judges' Charter of Basic Rights and Freedoms.***

Or the Judges' Charter, for short.

In order to decide what our most basic entitlements are, I will need to discuss the Human Rights Act and human rights in general. I suppose, in discussing human rights, I will be defending the Act indirectly. This is unavoidable as many of our most basic entitlements already exist today in the form of human rights. Hence, if my discussion helps to convince some readers that, actually, human rights are a good thing.... so be it.

The most basic entitlements that people are born with can indeed be described as human rights and freedoms. Freedom from slavery is one example. Freedom of thought is another. At a very minimum, we are all entitled to these most basic of liberties. No decent politician would presume to say otherwise. Would you vote for any politician who did?

Unfortunately, though, different politicians hold different views about which of our rights are 'human' (so must be upheld) and which rights are more like privileges (so can be revoked).

No political party wishes to bring back slavery, nor to control our thoughts, but there is considerable disagreement on matters such as privacy and the right to a family life. These legal rights are enjoyed today by everyone in Britain. They are also taken for granted. But, should we give these rights up so that some criminals might be captured quicker, and some illegal immigrants deported easier?

I am certain that, when the dreaded referendum comes, I will be ticking 'no' in the box next to this question. In the meantime, the purpose of my book is to convince readers, including the most senior judges in Britain, that some of our rights, yours and mine, are much too important to lie at the mercy of tabloid reporters.

Some of our rights must be protected from politicians who would dare to tinker with them. Thus, I wish to propose a new way of guarding the most basic rights and freedoms that are enjoyed by Britons today.... but not for much longer if this present Government prevails.

What exactly is the Judges' Charter?

It is a document which spells out, in simple and plain words, all your most basic entitlements as a person – which no one can ever deprive you of.

The judges could use this document in court as a 'yardstick' to check that politicians and other officials are not going too far in their work and trampling on our freedom. Thus, if any Act of Parliament were to offend the basic principles laid down by the Judges' Charter (say, by dispensing with the need to have trials), then the Act would not be recognised as a proper law in Britain. The same goes for any decision of a government minister, or public official, which turns out to be unfair to lots of people.

Surely, this charter could not be used to inflict harm; it could only be an instrument for good. It would stop Britain from ever becoming a police state – or at least, a harsh place where people are forced to obey the Government, even when it is acting unfairly.

Let me assure you: the need for this simple checklist is real. Even if you are sick to death of reading about 'human rights for criminals' and such, it is still vital that at least *some* of the rights contained in the Human Rights Act are protected for you, me and everybody.... always. Otherwise, without having some basic entitlements to count on in court, we will be handing politicians in Parliament the absolute power to decide what is good for us.

Whilst some people may be comfortable with this idea, I am not, for as Lord Acton wisely put it: "Power tends to corrupt, and absolute power corrupts absolutely."

In terms of corruption, we saw how politicians of all the main parties were recently embarrassed by an expenses scandal, proving that they are in politics mainly for themselves, not us. That aside, there are many examples of local councils, and other public bodies, taking decisions which the courts have not been shy to condemn – using strong terms such as "blatant abuse of power."

The exact words may differ from judgment to judgment, but the need for people to sue an authority for over-stepping its bounds is now a common thing indeed.

In the past, the courts have even denounced certain police officers as "liars" – proving that nobody is beyond suspicion of corruption.

Clearly, therefore, no one can be trusted to always know what is good for us. Any person or body wielding public power must be willing to be checked from time to time – and by an independent judge, not a fellow politician or similar, reliable official.

This seems like a reasonable safeguard which no public servant should object to. Yet, in Britain, our system is designed so that the higher an official climbs, the less stringent his checks become.

Ultimately one reaches Parliament, the apex of British power, where the only real scrutiny that occurs is handled by the politicians themselves. This is not reassuring, especially since politicians were caught skimming from the public purse. And, if that were not bad enough, it emerged how, on the eve of this scandal breaking, they colluded together to try and pass a last-minute law which would have made MPs' expenses a state secret forever.

In sum, we can no longer assume that politicians act with the purest intentions. The time has come, my friends, for us to wake up and see what is happening.

According to daily tabloid *The Sun,* David Cameron intends to 'rip up' the Human Rights Act, thus revoking the individual, legal rights enjoyed by us all today. I suggest, Cameron's motives for wishing to do so must be questioned, for he too has been tarred by corruption of late and has all but admitted ill-judgment.

In the meantime, before the Human Rights Act is shredded, if the judges of Britain choose to adopt the Judges' Charter, this will create a simple-but-vital kind of 'higher' law which nobody can tinker with, not even the Prime Minister.

Our most basic rights would be safe forever.

Who am I to propose this charter?

Well, I can assure you that I am not a lawyer, although I have nothing against lawyers. Nor do I work in politics, although I try to take an interest. Really, I am just a concerned citizen who happens to have studied law. I have also spent some time doing 'hands-on' human rights work.

In America I assisted a lawyer with death penalty appeals, and in West Africa I helped to campaign for women's rights and freedom of information. And, in both these places, my eyes were opened by the sheer injustice that I saw. That is why on returning home, I felt compelled to write this book, as though it were my civic duty – like stepping out to vote, or sitting on a jury.

Right now, this modest-sized work is the best contribution I can make to Britain: our vibrant, democratic island which I am proud to belong to.

History shows that many of the greatest, most influential books to have graced our libraries were written, not by learned scholars, but men and women of humble means who confronted injustice with the word, not the sword. My aim here is to follow in that same, bold tradition.

I speak for Britons who, like myself, want only to live with the minimum possible fuss and the maximum possible power to pursue our idea of happiness. That, my friends, is the true essence of freedom, and it should not be looked upon as a prize. Freedom is the birthright of us all, not just a lucky few.

I speak for people I know who must work two or three jobs, yet cannot say for sure if the rent will be there next month. Where is the justice in that?

I speak for children in our state school system whose potential may be high, but whose chances are low due to a failure to protect the vulnerable from vicious, daily bullying at the hands and tongues of less dedicated pupils. Where is the justice in that?

I speak for Britain's senior citizens who end their days in our care homes, yet, far from receiving the tender care that is promised, they find themselves subject to degrading treatment by callous staff who couldn't care less. Where is the justice in that?

I speak for people I know who ended up being convicted of a crime, not because they are evil, but because they failed to show deference to an egotistical police officer who came wading into a delicate, emotionally-charged situation, boots first. Where is the justice in that?

I speak for British Muslims who do not wish to be associated with terror-preaching radicals, any more than catholics wish to be associated with child-molesting priests.

I speak for committed gay couples who want their union to be called a marriage, not a 'civil partnership' – which implies there is something unholy about their decision to grow old together.

And I speak for Britain's disabled people, whose strong, alert minds resent the presumption of incapability which has yet to be eradicated from our society.

Something is most definitely wrong when all this injustice (and more) surrounds us, yet our Prime Minister is talking about reducing legal rights for the individual, not increasing them. Still, whilst I claim to speak for many, not everyone will agree with me.

As a person with a disability from a poor, working-class background, I would not have a law degree today, nor would I be writing this book, were it not for progressive, left-wing policies which enabled me to get up and get educated when I felt the desire to learn. Thus, my world view has been shaped by experience. I can make no apology for that.

As far as politics go, I would tend to vote for the Labour Party, although I accept that no major party can lay claim to a perfect track record on defending our rights and freedoms.

Labour may have introduced the Human Rights Act, but not all of its decisions accorded with human rights in the years which followed. Likewise, the Conservatives may be working to abolish the Act today, but there would be no Act at all if Winston Churchill, a Conservative politician, had not first championed the European Convention on Human Rights.

Ultimately, therefore, I think that Britain has both parties to thank for the freedom she enjoys.... even though that freedom is at grave risk today.

About this book ...

In getting my idea across, I wanted to avoid the 'stuffiness' of other legal and political writings. I want my words to be read and understood by as many people as possible, not just lawyers and law students. Therefore, I have kept legal terms to a minimum and tried to explain things thoroughly. I have also avoided using footnotes; instead, there is a reference section at the end of the book where you can find further information relating to each part.

The book begins with an introduction in which I discuss my idea for the Judges' Charter and some legal concepts which underlie it. These concepts were necessary to include as knowing them will help you to better understand my discussion. Rest assured, the information is not too technical, and I have kept it as light and topical as possible.

The rest of the introduction then deals with bad myths about human rights which, it seems, have doomed the Human Rights Act to failure. The myths I tackle range from 'anarchy in schools' to 'terrorists among us' – all caused by human rights, apparently.

By addressing the myths, I aim to expose the power that the tabloid press has to pervert public opinion. Even if you choose to skip the more technical stuff, at least read about the myths, for the day is surely coming when you will be asked to vote 'yes' in a referendum to abolish the Human Rights Act; hence, you should know all the facts before you tick that fatal box.

Those who enjoy the topical style of my introduction may wish to read the book's afterword, in which I discuss why I am against the Conservative proposal for a 'British' Bill of Rights – which they plan to replace our Human Rights Act with.

The afterword is followed by a timeline of key events which map the development of rights in Britain. I include this partly for David Cameron and his party, whose knowledge of British history seems to fade around the Second World War. Hopefully, this timeline will show the Conservatives that human rights are indeed British rights. And you might be interested, too.

The main part of this book is my petition to The Justices of The Supreme Court. Here I speak directly to Their Lordships of the need to take constitutional action on all our behalves. The petition concludes with my draft outline of the Judges' Charter, which I hope Their Lordships will take and apply to court cases in future; that way, whatever happens to the Human Rights Act, we will always have this 'safety net' of basic entitlements to fall back on.

With the courts upholding the Judges' Charter, politicians of all parties could aim to provide more, but they will never be able to give us less.... nor should they want to.

History has shown how injustice triumphs when good people do nothing. Perhaps it is too late to prevent the

Human Rights Act being revoked, but it is not too late for concerned citizens to take a stand on which hard-won rights they refuse to let go of as our nation slumbers.

This is my stand against the oppression I see coming.

What will be yours?

"I think it's one of the great glories of our judicial system that the political background of judges has always been regarded as absolutely, completely irrelevant."

– Michael Howard, former Leader of the Conservative Party, speaking in 2011

Introduction

In 2009, I submitted a short piece of writing to a current affairs magazine. The magazine was inviting answers to an important question:

'Should Britain have a written Bill of Rights?'

For those who are unsure what this means, a Bill of Rights is a document laying down all your rights and freedoms which the Government must respect, or else face legal action. It is different from an Act of Parliament. A Bill of Rights is more powerful; it can never be taken away, nor altered, by politicians acting on a whim.

At present, 2012, Britain has no Bill of Rights. Instead, we have the Human Rights Act which is the next best thing.... or not, depending whether you happen to think that every person has basic, minimal entitlements which the State has a duty to respect – even where the law has been broken.

When I joined this debate, I was studying for my law degree and had not long returned from West Africa, having volunteered to do some work for a human rights organisation.

The passion for defending peoples' rights had thus taken root in my heart. More pressingly, though, having witnessed some flagrant abuses abroad, I was starting to think about the way our rights are protected at home. I wondered if our own rights, yours and mine, are any better protected than the rights belonging to our third-world neighbours. And it turns out *no* – they're not.

It seems that in Africa and Europe alike, politicians have personal agendas which often conflict with the rights of ordinary, individual citizens – the voters who elect them. Moreover, on both these continents, and in America too, a political party may start with good, poetic ideals (for which it gets picked to govern), but the party is soon forced to compromise as society is confronted by difficult issues, a prime example being terrorism. For all politicians, therefore, staying in power means staying popular.... whatever the cost may be.

And so began my project, with a probing question of my own:

Are politicians the best people to be keeping watch over our most basic liberties?

It took me some pondering, but at last, the answer to this question shone clear through my mind. It occurred to me that initially, in the raw stages of democracy, our elected representatives (called politicians, or MPs) are well-placed to decide what rights we should have. This is because our representatives come to power by trying to make the world a better place.

In the run-up to elections, politicians want the best for society, at least according to their vision, so they will promise the people certain things as of right – and we, the people, shall answer with our vote. Such is the nature of democracy: our votes may bring us rights.

Not every right can be described as a vital 'human' one, though.

Some rights are more like privileges and can be taken away from us in time, as new politicians, and new ideas, replace the old. For instance, the right to free milk at school (abolished 1971). Doubtless, this right was of great benefit to children; especially children from poor families. However, this right was not deemed vital enough to be described as a 'human' one, so despite loud protests, it could not be saved from repeal.

Another example was the right to a tax break for all married couples (abolished 2000), which was really a privilege more than a right. Hence, it is often the case that when we claim to have the right to something, in fact, we have no more than a privilege for the time being – to be enjoyed until further notice.

On the other hand, some rights are quite different to privileges and belong apart, in a special league of their own. Some rights are fundamental, meaning that we are born with them; we can feel these rights in our bones. When a fundamental right is breached, it hurts, just as it hurts if a bone is broken.

Our fundamental rights go beyond mere privileges, as the very act of taking them away would be to assault humanity itself. Examples include:

The right to get married.
The right to have children.
The right to own property.
The right to some privacy.
The right to free speech.
The right to fair treatment.
The right to be safe from torture.

Rights such as these ought to offend nobody; they are harmless, and can indeed be described as the 'human' kind. Yet, one has only to open a newspaper to find that, in fact, governments around the world object to these rights and refuse to respect them fully.

In America, gay couples are denied the benefits of ordinary married life. In China, couples who have more than one child are breaking the law. In South Africa, families can suddenly find that their land has been sold from under them. And in Britain, it will soon be possible for police and local councils to invade our privacy by reading the e-mails and text messages of any person, at any time, with the simple push of a button.

In countries where there is democracy, however, a person who is badly affected by such policies can use special laws to challenge their government. These special laws are what we tend to call human rights, but they can also be called civil liberties, or civil rights, or constitutional freedoms.

Whatever we happen to call them, these basic rights are the bare minimum that all people should be able to expect. A government may create policies which violate these rights, but the people living in a democracy do not have to stand for it; they can use the law to fight for change.

I suggest that in a fair society, the minimum entitlements which all people can expect to receive are non-negotiable. The survival of such basic rights should not (and must not) depend on the whim of any party sitting in Parliament. Nor should it depend on public opinion, even, as this would open the door to mob rule.

My argument is that, once declared by the democratic process, it is not politicians, nor us, but surely *the judges* who become responsible for shielding our most basic rights from assault – even if the assault comes from politicians, old or new.

If you think about it, this idea is not unreasonable; it makes perfect sense. Ask yourself: should your right to privacy be treated the same as a tax break? And is free speech the same as free milk?

Surely not, I say, for these basic rights never go out of vogue; they're universal. In fact, with something so universal, no decent, prudent parliament would act to enshrine it in law.... but only until the next election. That would indeed be a shallow, pointless gesture to make.

Instead, common decency dictates that such basic entitlements, when enshrined, are enshrined for the good of everyone, always. And later, if some politicians try to tinker with this most basic law, there must come a point when it falls to someone (other than politicians) to command aloud:

"In the name of freedom, stop what you are doing!"

But why the judges? After all, judges in Britain are not elected, so why trust them to be the guardians of our most dearly valued liberties?

The answer is because judges act for the long-term, whilst politicians must live for the moment. And in their work, politicians must strive for power, whilst judges strive only for justice. In sum, judges have nothing to gain by tinkering with our rights, but politicians will tinker if doing so could help to win votes.

So, it does seem that judges are best-placed to make the wise, dispassionate decisions whenever voters are willing, quite suddenly, to sacrifice all our traditional liberties – usually in response to some issue which politicians and tabloids are exaggerating.

In America, the top judges of that democratic country have the power to strike-down any law which is found to violate the basic rights of citizens. This practice is copied today by the judges of South Africa, Germany, Canada and many other places.

Even within the UK, Northern Ireland has expressed her own desire to move in this direction. Hence, the time has truly come for Britain to catch up with the rest of the democratic world by having some kind of 'higher' law in place, which no politician can tinker with. This higher law would safeguard personal freedom, yours and mine, forever.

Ignited, three years ago, by thoughts such as these, I penned my piece for the said magazine. And, to my delight, it was picked for publication.

With 150 words at my disposal, I had written:

> Britain has no constitution – just a precarious gentleman's agreement that is subject to the greatest of all evils: unfettered discretion. However, because of this, our laws derive their legitimacy, not from Parliament's ability to legislate, but from the willingness of the courts to apply that legislation.
>
> Dicey conceded this when he defined law as "any rule which will be enforced by the courts." Dicey did not define law as 'any rule made by Parliament', for Parliament alone cannot enforce its enactments; it depends on the courts for its rules to work.
>
> Therefore, it is perfectly conceivable that our highest judges could use their position, as officers of the State, to declare an entrenched, true Bill of Rights for citizens; a document prescribing minimum standards of human dignity to be observed by all.... always.
>
> If there is hope for peoples' rights, it lies in our judges, not our executive-led Parliament.

My friends, I continue to stand by this ideal. I believe, with all my liberal heart, that if positive action is not taken soon, and by judges rather than politicians, then the freedom 'train' will be de-railed in Britain, leaving each one of us stranded; cut-off from the full protection of the courts with only a distant, disinterested MP to write to whenever our liberties have been breached.

The day draws near when tabloid propaganda and political spin will put an end to freedom as we know it. And, worst of all: we, the people of Britain, will cheer when that day comes.

I see this happening and it scares me. Good people I know are ready to vote away their fundamental, legal rights in a referendum, and gladly at that, if it will bring some rough treatment to a few unsavoury villains who deserve to get their comeuppance. This is because, thanks to the tabloid press, the word 'rights' has become synonymous with criminals in many peoples' minds.

I will venture that many white, British-born, law-abiding citizens think the State will never seek to bother them, nor their family, nor their property. Thus, these people take no comfort in having the full power of the courts on their side, armed and ready, just in case. But oh, how woefully complacent!

Right now, at this moment, a handful of government officials are planning to yank the reins on British liberty, once and for all, for all of us. This elite few are seeking, not to abolish our rights entirely, but to harness and control them for selfish ends. They mean to re-write our democracy under a so-called 'British' Bill of Rights.

If they succeed, which looks very likely now, we will have many rights in theory but few rights in practice. Our freedom to question authority, of any kind, will be forever tempered. Our power to challenge ill-treatment, of any sort, will be diminished.

Make no mistake about it: for every man, woman and child in Britain, this is a serious step with lasting consequences.

Because we are living in relative peacetime, the personal freedom that each one of us enjoys, fought for by Winston Churchill, is largely taken for granted. But we have so much to lose.

That is why, I suggest, certain rights that we enjoy today must be removed from the political arena and scribed, for all to behold, upon the very walls of our courts. Some of our rights must be secured within the minds of the judges, forever, and thus made immune to the tinkering of Parliament.

The time for this to happen is now, before the Conservatives can revoke all our rights, water them down, then restore them to us under a 'British' Bill of Rights which will replace our Human Rights Act, permanently. You can read more about this in my afterword, in which I argue against the Conservative proposal for a 'British' Bill of Rights.

Meanwhile, let there be no doubt: through the words of my petition, I aim to convince our most senior judges, The Justices of The Supreme Court, that constitutional action must be taken by them on behalf of everyone in Britain.

I shall petition Their Lordships for a modest (not radical) reform, as when they declared the Practice Statement of 1966 – which empowered our Supreme Court to depart from previous rulings whenever a case demands changes to the law, rather than having to wait for Parliament to make those changes.

For readers without the benefit of a law degree or much political knowledge, I must now explain some concepts that are key to my later arguments.

To round-off this introduction, I will then tackle six bad myths about human rights. These myths were started by politicians and fuelled by the tabloid press. I will discuss these, not so much to defend the Human Rights Act, but to reveal how tabloid writers have the power to distort anything they dislike – be it human rights today, or the Judges' Charter tomorrow.

So here are some insights from my studies.

I hope you will find them interesting.

The Separation of Powers

In my magazine piece, I refer to the three branches of state, also known as the three powers: Parliament, the executive and the judges. You should know what each 'branch' does, not just so you can read my petition to the judges, but so you will better understand political news in general.

Parliament is the law-making body, or legislative branch, which consists of the Queen, the House of Lords and, most importantly, the House of Commons. It is in the Commons that our elected MPs debate new legislation and vote on its passage.

A proposed law is called a 'bill' (not to be confused with a Bill of Rights), and a bill becomes an Act of Parliament when it passes through both Houses and is signed by the Queen. Acts of Parliament (also called 'statutes') are the highest source of law in Britain.

The executive branch is the Government led by the Prime Minister. Note: the word 'government' can be used in a more general sense to refer to the overall running of the country.

Besides governing and setting the policy agenda, the Prime Minister and most (if not all) of his ministers also sit as elected MPs. Thus, the executive branch is fused with Parliament. Essentially, this enables the Government of the day to turn its policy ideas into new laws.... and scrap current laws that it does not like.

The police and army are examples of executive bodies. They must do as the Government commands; hence, they come under the executive branch of state.

The judges, also called the judicial branch, decide the outcome of cases brought before the courts. Historically, the judges were deciding cases before Parliament had been established, so they were once the makers of law in Britain. Today, however, judges are not required to make law but must interpret the meaning of legislation in the cases they hear. The precise way that an Act of Parliament is interpreted in a higher court will set a precedent for lower courts to follow. This is known as case law, or common law.

In effect, judges still make law by 'reading between the lines' to cover new situations not explicitly mentioned in an Act. It can be argued that this is a crucial function of judges, otherwise, anarchy might result from disgruntled citizens taking matters into their own hands if an Act of Parliament fails to cover their exact problem.

Parliament can only legislate in broad terms; it cannot be expected to foresee every possible dispute that may arise between people. On the other hand, judges deal with real cases that come before the courts, so they can see how the law is working in practice.

In certain areas of the law that Parliament has chosen not to legislate on very much, such as contract law, ancient decisions of our courts continue to be regarded as the correct legal rules to follow.

The separation-of-powers means, for most purposes, that judges enjoy complete independence from the other two branches of state. This independence is vital for a healthy democracy, as cases often come before the courts in which the Government holds an interest. Corruption would thrive if government ministers were able to influence the outcome of cases. Citizens finding themselves aggrieved by state action would never be able to get justice if our judges were 'in the pocket' of ministers and other officials.

The independence of judges is especially important when you consider that the other two branches of state, Parliament and Government, are fused together – practically becoming the same body, depending on how many elected seats the Government can lay claim to. A strong majority of seats will ensure that the biggest party 'runs' Parliament, so to speak. In that situation, the courts may act as a check on the absolute power of the Prime Minister.

Of course, the General Election serves as the ultimate check. If the Prime Minister and his Government are doing badly, the public can vote him out of office. However, the public gets this chance only once every five years, so the risk of losing votes is not enough to keep the Government in line if it chooses (bit by bit, day by day) to encroach on peoples' freedom. Thus, some other kind of check is needed in the short-term, between elections.

This is where judges come in.

To quote Professor Griffith: "Traditionally, judges are thought of as the defenders of the rights of individuals from attack by public authorities." Hence, despite a scary image that is often portrayed in films, judges do not exist simply to send people off to prison! Judges are "at one and the same time, the protectors of personal rights, and the preservers of law and order."

Reinforcing the independence of judges, legislation now makes it illegal for any minister to try to influence a judge's decision. Also, judges' salaries are controlled by an independent body, and no senior judge can be sacked from office except if they should commit a crime or other serious misconduct. So judges are free to make their decisions without fear of upsetting the State. In fact, judges are officers of the State – every bit as much as government ministers and MPs.

"There is no doubt" says Professor Griffith, "about the importance of judges in our society. Their professional eminence, their influence on the development of the law and the extent of their powers confirm that judges maintain their position as part of established authority."

The bottom line:

Judges do not have to do what politicians tell them to.

Constitutions: Written and Unwritten

A constitution refers to the system of rules and principles by which a country is governed. For example, the rules governing elections and how voting takes place will come under constitutional law. The fundamental rights of citizens also form part of a country's constitution.

In some countries, such as America, the constitution is literally spelled-out, rule by rule, in a written document called the Constitution (capital C). In Britain, instead of a written constitution, we have an arrangement – otherwise called the 'unwritten' (small c) constitution.

The former Justice Secretary, Jack Straw, summed it up nicely. He said that our constitution exists "in hearts and minds and habits as much as in law."

That sounds like a romantic idea, but what does it actually mean?

Well, putting it simply, some of Britain's constitutional rules are legal; that is, contained in Acts of Parliament and ancient decisions of our courts. But many of our constitutional rules are informal practices established over centuries, known as conventions.

A good example is the convention that government ministers take full responsibility for the work of their department, even though, in reality, the minister cannot be involved in every decision and must rely on special advisers.

Where public crisis results from a serious blunder, the minister in charge is expected to resign. This should ensure that ministers stay vigilant and do not become lazy in office, handing their most trusted duties off to the bureaucracy. It should also prevent ministers being able to duck responsibility by blaming someone else when things go wrong.

In practice, however, few ministers regard this convention as binding. History shows that whilst some ministers have resigned over serious failings, others have made excuses and refused to go. Where a minister refuses to resign (and the Prime Minister refuses to sack him), there is nothing the courts can do because the rule is not a legal one. It is more of a 'habit' than a law.... and not a very addictive habit, I must say.

Our 'unwritten' constitution is made up of many conventions like this. Those intended to control politicians are especially flexible. As stated, though, some constitutional rules are legally binding – meaning that, when broken, these rules can be enforced by the courts.

The part of any written constitution which sets out the fundamental rights of citizens is known as the Bill of Rights. This document is most definitely a legal one. In Britain, the Human Rights Act (passed by the Labour Party) serves as our makeshift Bill of Rights. However, it is possible for a country to have a proper Bill of Rights without having a full-fledged constitution to go with it.

From the ordinary citizen's perspective, a Bill of Rights is useful because the citizen can quickly learn what his or her rights are by reading this document, either on paper or online.

A Bill of Rights is easier to understand than an Act of Parliament because, being a constitutional document, it is framed with the citizen in mind, whereas an Act is drafted *by* lawyers *for* lawyers.

Most importantly, though: once a country's Bill of Rights is enshrined in writing, it becomes the highest, most sacred law in the land. Even the President or Prime Minister is bound to obey this document and cannot alter it without the peoples' permission – usually obtained by a public referendum.

By contrast, an Act of Parliament can be altered or revoked at any time, without having to consult the people directly. Therefore, unlike an Act of Parliament, a Bill of Rights is said to be 'entrenched' or 'embedded' within the structure of government.

The bottom line:

A Bill of Rights is permanent, but an Act of Parliament is not.

The Supremacy of Parliament

It has long been accepted that, since Britain does not have a written constitution, the highest laws we have are the Acts passed by our Parliament. Parliament is thus seen to be the sovereign law-maker, meaning its rules are supreme.

In 1885, our most cherished constitutional writer, Professor Albert Venn Dicey, wrote: "Parliament has the right to make or unmake any law whatever; and further, no person or body is recognised by the law as having a right to override or set aside the legislation of Parliament."

Today, the UK's membership of the European Union means that Parliament must comply with Regulations and Directives which are handed-down to EU member states. These rules do not always accord with what the British people want – for instance, the abolition of pounds and ounces in favour of kilograms.

EU rules can sometimes clash with Acts of Parliament, meaning the Act must be amended to comply. It can thus be said that an EU rule overrides a rule made by Parliament, so Dicey's words are no longer true.

On the other hand, Parliament joined the EU voluntarily by passing a law in 1972. And, when put to a vote, the people supported EU membership by a referendum in 1975. Thus, it can also be argued that membership is in accordance with the sovereign will, and therefore, the supremacy of Parliament remains intact – even if some politicians are unhappy.

Parliament has also agreed to respect our human rights. This is yet another limitation on the supremacy of Parliament today.

However, laws made by Parliament will 'write over' the decisions of our courts – known as case law. The law on rape provides a good example of this.

In 1992, there was no Act of Parliament which made it illegal for a husband to rape his wife. When such a case was brought to court for the first time, Their Lordships ruled that the husband could be found guilty. This decision then stood as the law for a while.

Later, in 2003, Parliament passed the Sexual Offences Act which recognised the crime of marital rape. The Act has overwritten the case law because Parliament is supreme. Thus, the judges have no further say on this issue and must apply the Sexual Offences Act to all rape cases in future.

The bottom line:

Parliament is the supreme power, but Parliament has chosen to put limits on this power – such as the need to respect human rights.

Judicial Review

Judges have given themselves a necessary licence to examine secondary legislation, such as local council parking laws, which are passed outside of Parliament using power that has been delegated by Parliament.

Delegating the power to make 'minor' laws allows MPs the time to debate more high-profile laws that are proposed. However, as secondary legislation is not subject to the rigorous checking and debate that occurs in Parliament, it is possible for power to be misapplied – resulting in bad law which citizens can fall foul of. Where this happens, an aggrieved citizen may petition the court for 'judicial review' to have the bad law annulled.

Secondary legislation includes regulations created by ministers, such as the Housing Benefit Regulations, and judges can review these too. Also, any decision taken by a public body, such as the National Health Service, is subject to review.

In countries where there is a written constitution, Acts of Parliament (or Acts of Congress, etc) can be reviewed by judges and declared void if the Act conflicts with the Constitution.

In Britain, Parliament is the highest source of law we have, so judges cannot void an Act as they would void a bad parking law. At most, an Act may be declared incompatible with human rights if it conflicts with the Human Rights Act. Even then, a declaration of incompatibility serves only to draw Parliament's attention to a problem; Parliament is not obliged to fix it.

History shows that judicial review is a source of tension for governments – even in Britain, where the power is greatly restricted. This tension is generally seen as positive, though; the sure sign of a healthy democracy.

To quote the late, great, Tom Bingham, former Lord Chief Justice: "There are countries in the world where all judges' decisions find favour with the Government, but they are not places where one would wish to live."

The bottom line:

If the State does something to upset a citizen, the citizen may take the State to court.

At first brush, this information may seem irrelevant to ordinary, everyday people. Who's really bothered, right?

And yet, these points will be known to anyone, anywhere, who has ever had to challenge a serious injustice of any kind. These points are the machine parts of Britain and America. And many other places aspire to have a system like ours. In practice, however, many places fail to make it work as well as it could – including Britain and America, occasionally.

Martin Luther King understood this stuff as he challenged White America to make good on her creed of equality.

The first Prime Minister of Ghana, Kwame Nkrumah, understood this stuff as he sat in a colonial prison, dreaming of independence for his British-gripped land.

In Cuba, the Ladies in White understand this stuff as they march in silence each Sunday, protesting against the conviction of their husbands – imprisoned by a communist regime for daring to speak their liberal minds.

And in Britain, the parents of Derek Bentley came to know this stuff as they fought to save their son's innocent neck from a death sentence that would break it. Whilst nothing would keep Derek from meeting this tragic end, the penalty of death would shortly be abolished.

Hence, no system of laws is perfect, but where there is democracy, at least, there is hope. As history continues to show: the wheels of justice turn slowly, but from the fibres of democracy they sometimes spin gold.

Before tackling the myths about human rights, there are just two further points which ought to be discussed: the rule of law and the promise of democracy.

The Rule of Law

For farmers and pharmacists, teachers and plumbers: the State is the State and it works the same for everyone. No one is above the law, including politicians and judges.

This hallowed principle is known as the rule of law. It applies, without exception, to every being and body. To put it in the words of Thomas Fuller (1733): "Be ye ever so high, still the law is above you."

The rule of law is a great thing to cite in a speech, or in court, when arguing that a government minister (or some public body) is not obeying the law as ordinary citizens must. *'He thinks he's above the law!'* we might say. On its own, though, the rule of law does not guarantee any rights.

In Nazi Germany, for instance, it could be said that all citizens obeyed the law dutifully, from the lowest factory worker to the highest ranking official. By following Hitler's decrees, Germany observed the rule of law.

The trouble was, Nazi law permitted the torture and murder of any suspected traitor – in other words, any person with a mind to speak out. Thus, the law may have been obeyed, but it favoured the Government overwhelmingly. In Nazi Germany, 'rule of law' meant 'having no rights.'

The great judge, Lord Bingham, would have disagreed with me here.

In his book, *The Rule of Law*, Bingham argues that certain fundamental rights must go hand-in-hand with this principle. In other words, in places where governments truly observe the rule of law (unlike Nazi Germany), certain fundamental rights will be respected naturally. Bingham seems to suggest, therefore, that in a fair society like ours, some rights go almost without saying – and always will, no matter what happens to the Human Rights Act.

Lord Bingham argues that the rights encapsulated within the rule of law include the right to a fair trial and the prohibition of torture, plus family life, privacy, education and free expression.

Whilst I wish this could be so, I think it is too fanciful to be true. History shows that, in reality, governments claim always to observe the rule of law.... even as they are violating it. Hence, if Lord Bingham's high standards were suddenly to apply, no government on Earth would be able to claim this virtue with a straight face.

In their response to terrorism, for example, Britain and America have ignored the most basic of rights in the interests of national security. Both countries pledge faithful adherence to the rule of law, yet both have committed acts which are illegal (and shameful) by common standards. Alas, much tyranny has occurred under the banner of freedom and justice.

This is the stark dilemma which Bingham's ideal overlooks: governments will usually find a way to justify their illegal actions. The American prisons at Guantanamo Bay provide a good illustration of this.

Standing in communist Cuba, more than 90 miles from American soil, these military camps hold hundreds of suspects, purchased for cash from foreign governments (or else simply kidnapped), who have been imprisoned without charge and brutally tortured for information.

The torture of these men was specifically authorised by President George W. Bush, who refers to this in his memoirs as "enhanced interrogation." In his book, he further admits:

"[...] CIA experts drew up a list of techniques. At my direction, lawyers conducted a careful review. Waterboarding, a process of simulated drowning, was no doubt a tough procedure, but medical experts assured the CIA that it did no lasting harm. The enhanced interrogation programme complied with all laws, including those that ban torture."

Now, because the prisons have been built in Cuba, no American judge is able to rule on whether this so-called 'technique' is legal. Instead, we have the word of a politician that "simulated drowning" does not count as torture. So technically, America has violated no rights and the rule of law stands unbroken.

Meanwhile, suspects at Guantanamo continue to exist in limbo, never knowing when, or if, their ordeal will end. They are denied a trial because of concerns that secret intelligence might be exposed. It is anyone's guess how useful this intelligence has been, but we know that Guantanamo was torturing suspects for over three years when the 7/7 bombings happened in London. Thus, the 'intelligence' did nothing to help Britain.

In effect, America has created a special class of suspects who can be treated differently from every suspected robber, rapist and murderer on American soil.

Britain did a similar thing during the conflict with Northern Ireland, and the former Labour Government used the Belmarsh Prison in London for holding terror suspects without charge – until our judges ruled this illegal.

Even more disturbingly, *The Guardian* has recently confirmed seeing evidence that Britain is complicit in the use of torture to extract information from Guantanamo prisoners and suspects being held at secret prisons abroad.

I suggest, the American prisons in Cuba, and all secret prisons, are an affront to the rule of law, and living proof that no fundamental rights can ever be guaranteed by this principle alone.

At a minimum, therefore, observing the rule of law should mean doing what the law says, whoever you happen to be, and not being able to pick and choose when the law shall apply. This seems to be the least controversial meaning. Yet, even expressed like this, in such a simple manner, it is a goal which no government may ever achieve fully.

I believe that any country can observe the rule of law without respecting human rights, but no country can respect human rights without observing the rule of law. The rule of law is what enables citizens to enforce their rights against the Government, but only if the law happens to recognise rights to begin with.

To quote the late Lord Diplock, a judge of equal rank to Bingham:

"[...] When the meaning of statutory words is plain and unambiguous, it is not for judges to invent fancied ambiguities as an excuse for failing to give effect to plain meaning, just because they consider the consequences to be immoral. It endangers the rule of law if judges provide their own preferred amendments to statutes."

With the utmost respect to Lord Diplock, a judge working under Hitler might have spoken these exact same words. His Lordship's message, however well-meaning, is clear: when the law is precise, a judge must apply it.... even if it seems immoral to do so. And certainly, this position is one which favours authority over the citizen.

In their speeches, British politicians (especially Conservatives) tend to exalt the rule of law as though nothing else matters in a just society. It sounds impressive, but as we can see: the rule of law is not enough on its own to prevent tyranny.

What also matters are human rights, yours and mine, for these are the special ingredient which make the law good. Thus, without at least a sprinkling of human rights, even for humans we wish to punish, the rule of law becomes an empty gesture; it benefits only the Government, and certainly does not guarantee our freedom.

The bottom line:

The law can be used to protect peoples' rights, but their rights must be enshrined in writing, not presumed in theory.

The Promise of Democracy

It is fair to say that, in Britain, most people trust the Government – or at least, they have faith that the Government is not trying to hurt us or exploit our weaker position. And, in some ways, I am inclined to agree with this. Ultimately, though, politics is about popularity (winning votes); it is not always about doing the right thing.

For centuries, Britain has claimed to be a democracy, meaning a place where government is of the people, by the people and for the people. However, for any nation, the mere act of saying this does not make it so. For instance, the Soviet Union held elections and claimed to be democratic, yet history records that place as a violent, communist dictatorship which imprisoned its good citizens behind borders, refusing to let them leave – even for a holiday. Hence, a democracy anywhere must be judged by its deeds, not by its words.

"No one pretends that democracy is perfect." said Winston Churchill. "Indeed, democracy is the worst form of government.... except for all those other forms that have been tried."

The trouble with democracy is that, quite often, if depriving a few will delight the many then majority rule prevails, for when push comes to shove, an appeased minority of voters cannot decide an election. Yet, if democracy is no more than keeping an insistent crowd happy, what makes it any better than mob rule? Instinct says that, surely, somehow, democracy has to be fairer than that.

Today, it is widely agreed that a democracy can be judged based on how well it allows the voice of minorities to be heard. Some might even argue that to be counted in a minority is the sacred hallmark of civil society. And any one of us could find ourselves in a minority, by the way, if we should ever choose to disagree with popular opinion. Being in a minority does not have to mean being gay, or disabled, or black, etc.

In his book, *On Liberty*, John Stuart Mill wrote: "If all mankind, minus one, were of a single opinion, and only one person were of the contrary opinion, mankind would be no more justified in silencing that one person than he, if he had the power, would be justified in silencing mankind."

Professor Dworkin distinguishes democracy like this: "A true democracy is a *communal* democracy, where majority decision is legitimate only within a community of equals – each individual guaranteed rights which no combination of other citizens can take away."

Such pearls of wisdom have helped to shape peoples' rights, but their sanctity has been eroded by selfish tinkerers through the years. I suggest, having fair and equal rights under the law is what makes the difference between a truly democratic society, and one where the mob prevails.

The bottom line:
Democracy means more than just voting.

Busting Corruption

Despite its dislike of human rights in general, and privacy in particular, the tabloid press can sometimes be good for holding ministers and politicians to account.

Thanks to freedom of information (a human right), newspapers were recently able to demand disclosure of MPs' expense accounts – resulting in a huge scandal.

The public was outraged to read about phantom mortgages and champagne, all funded by the taxpayer. On the day this story broke, I imagine there was much cursing in government about the right to information.... and the right to write about it!

In the 1980s, before Britain had freedom of information, the Thatcher Government prosecuted many people under the Official Secrets Act who dared to reveal sensitive facts to the public, even when the facts proved misconduct. Thus, Mrs Thatcher would never have tolerated the expenses scam being leaked; she would have used the law to prosecute any whistleblower.

It must therefore be said that whilst scandals are a bad thing, they demonstrate the power of human rights in a democracy. Where rights can burn bright, they starve corruption of the dark.

So, despite what tabloids are printing, human rights do not exist to coddle terrorists: they exist to bust corruption in our society and prevent injustice happening to ordinary people.

I will now address six prominent myths which could soon de-rail the movement. Again, I do this, not so much to defend the Human Rights Act, but to show you how tabloid propaganda is at work all around us. There are lessons to be learned from the daily scorn that is heaped upon this law.

Myth #1: "Only criminals benefit from human rights!"

This is false.

In general, criminal cases make better reading than civil ones. Human rights are thus more likely to be read about in the context of a grim murder trial rather than a compulsory land purchase, or the refusal to approve a child adoption application. This is partly why the Human Rights Act appears to be little more than a criminals' charter to so many people.

The other problem is that tabloids tend only to report the mere fact that a claim has been made under the Act, not whether the claim succeeds in court, or even gets to court. Thus, whenever a mischievous claim of some kind is put in, the public is led to believe that the claimant will definitely get what he has asked for, as though it is a foregone conclusion.

These types of stories cause outrage. And so, to set the record straight:

Prisoners do not have a human right to view pornography!

Nor do prisoners have a human right to a holiday.

Known paedophiles do not have a human right to keep their identities anonymous.

Police suspects do not have a human right to free cigarettes and takeaway meals.

Illegal immigrants do not have a human right to stay in Britain.... to look after a pet.

Use of CCTV and 'Wanted' posters does not breach offenders' human rights.

Gypsy travellers do not have a human right to set up camp wherever they please.

It seems, at least for now, that certain newspapers will continue to misrepresent crime stories in order to ensure profits and promote right-wing goals; in particular, the replacement of human rights with so-called 'British' ones. Given time, the reported "soft treatment of criminals" will arouse enough public anger to justify big changes to the law. I suggest, there lies the real aim behind all this propaganda.

If the Human Rights Act had been around in 1950, it would have saved the lives of two innocent men: Derek Bentley and Timothy Evans. Their British rights did not protect them from a British hangman when the British public was demanding blood. Hence, rather than accepting things blindly, more British people must try to question what they read.

The Human Rights Act protects the right to liberty for all. It protects the right to a fair trial for all. And for those of us who become victims of crime, the Act helps to ensure that we are treated with dignity by the justice system, or else we may sue the system where it fails in this regard – as sometimes happens, just as unfair trials still happen occasionally.

Whilst tabloids are busy calling the Human Rights Act a charter for criminals, they neglect to mention that there is an official Victims' Code, published by the Ministry of Justice, which you can discover online.

The Code (combined with a Witness Charter) sets out what victims can expect to happen from the moment they report a crime to police, and the support they will receive at each stage of the process. The rules provide, for instance, that suspects who choose to represent themselves in court are not allowed to question victims in certain types of cases, such as rape. Also, child witnesses are allowed to testify outside the courtroom via a live TV link.

So, despite what tabloids are printing, the legal process is not designed to abuse innocent victims whilst suspects are wrapped in cotton wool. Rather, the process aims to establish truth.

Every so often, a victim will have to answer some embarrassing questions in court. This is most regrettable as victims have already suffered enough by the time the trial occurs. But, to cite the creed of that iconic, much-loved character, Rumpole of the Bailey: a few questions must get asked before a fellow gets sent to prison. In other words, the accuser's story must be tested in court before it can be accepted as true.

Human rights aside, this seems to be a matter of basic fairness. Which one of us would choose to live in a society where a simple accusation is enough to end your liberty?

In addition to the Victims' Code, there is also a state-run compensation scheme. Any person who suffers injuries from a violent crime may claim compensation from the State. This money is paid to cover the reasonable cost of treatment, plus to compensate for loss of earnings and general pain and suffering. It is not even necessary for a criminal conviction to result.

So, despite what tabloids are printing, it is not only criminals who can claim money from the State when their rights have been violated. Victims can claim, too.

This is a delicate subject as public sympathy will tend to lie with the innocent victims of crime, not the persons accused of committing it. Whilst this is entirely understandable, we must all try to remember that in Britain, a suspect is innocent until proven guilty. That is the law of our land.

Winston Churchill suggested that the best test of a civilised society is how it chooses to treat its prisoners and those accused of committing crimes. "[...] A calm recognition of the rights of the accused, and even of convicted criminals, is proof of the stored-up strength of any nation" he said, speaking in Parliament.

Criminals may not deserve it, but showing them compassion, even the smallest amount, is what earns our society its moral righteousness.

Criminals are punished in our name: yours and mine. Should our name be made to stand for fairness? Or should it be used to justify barbaric treatment?

You must decide.

Myth #2: "Human rights are foreign-made laws!"

This is false.

The Human Rights Act is modelled after the European Convention on Human Rights. Despite its foreign-looking name, the Convention was created by Winston Churchill and a team of lawyers, mostly British. Among this team was Sir David Maxwell-Fyfe, a prominent lawyer who became the Conservative Home Secretary under Churchill.

When he championed the Convention in 1950, Churchill was the former British Prime Minister (shortly to be re-elected) and a Conservative politician. Thus, although the Human Rights Act was introduced by Labour in 1998, the Convention which underpins it is very much a Conservative creation.

Having defeated Hitler, Churchill was keen to make sure that the Nazi atrocities could never happen again. He also wanted to establish a new order throughout Europe, whereby governments must respect the rights of individuals. For the first time, Europe was becoming a community and this charter of rights helped to instil a community spirit – founded on British values.

The Human Rights Act, passed almost fifty years later, was merely the next step in giving these values the full protection of the British courts, so persons with a serious complaint against the Government would not be forced to leave home and travel to Strasbourg, taking their suitcase and legal case in search of justice.... after six years of waiting and expense. The Act took these nice principles and turned them into powerful legal rights, protected at home by the rule of law.

It must also be stated, perhaps cynically, that human rights are indeed British rights, for as history shows us: the Brits have rarely been part of anything they cannot control!

Britain signed-up to protect our human rights in 1951 (after writing them). It is therefore absurd to describe these principles as 'foreign laws' imposed on us against our will. What an insult to Churchill, our great wartime leader whose legacy was to defend British freedom – defying the will of a monstrous tyrant.

In Churchill's own words (addressing the Assembly in Strasbourg, 1949):

"[...] There is the question of human rights. We attach great importance to this. Once the foundation of human rights is agreed, we hope that a European Court might be set up, before which cases of violation of rights in our own nations might be brought to the judgment of the civilised world. Our nations would have subscribed beforehand to the process, and I have no doubt that public opinion in all these countries would press for action in accordance with this freely given decision."

Hence, let it never be forgotten that Winston Churchill was the Founding Father of human rights in Britain. For more on Churchill's legacy, see my timeline at the end of this book.

Myth #3: "Workers are suing employers over human rights!"

This is false.

Citizens may only use the Human Rights Act to sue the Government or a public body, such as the National Health Service, if it has breached a human right in some way.

The Act cannot be used to sue an employer, unless the employer happens to be a public body which has somehow breached a human right of one of its workers. An example might be a soldier who sues the army for degrading treatment.

The confusion started when David Cameron spoke of Labour's "health and safety, human rights culture." This quote became a catchphrase for insinuating that ordinary workers are suing their bosses for human rights payouts.

A rise in health and safety claims could be due to the growth of the internet, which has made information about the law accessible to everyone.

It has nothing to do with human rights, though.

Myth #4: "Human rights have curbed school discipline!"

This is false.

With regards to corporal punishment at school, it was the Conservatives in 1986 who first banned the caning of children by teachers. It is true that caning is not allowed today under the Human Rights Act, but it was outlawed in state schools for over thirteen years before the Act came into force.

With regards to the expulsion of unruly pupils, the Human Rights Act gives all children under sixteen the right to an education. This does not mean that a bad pupil cannot be expelled if he refuses to behave, although it does mean that the pupil must go somewhere – it is his right, but it is also the law, for the alternative is to unleash young, uneducated troublemakers on society.

Speaking from personal experience, I recall my early days at a state secondary school (before the Human Rights Act existed). It was dreadful. Discipline was weak. Many pupils came only to pick fights and disrupt classes. At the time, I would happily have seen them all expelled.... but where would they have gone? Which other school would be forced to take them in, and where would the bad kids from that other school go? You can see the dilemma.

The reluctance of schools to expel bad pupils has as much to do with protecting society as protecting the pupil's right to an education. Effective school discipline deserves its own debate. For now, though, I hope you will accept that human rights are not to blame for certain failings in the system at present.

Incidentally, whilst the tabloids are busy blaming human rights for the rise in bad behaviour, they neglect to mention how the Act has helped to address school bullying.

A school can now be sued if it 'turns a blind eye' to the degrading treatment of any pupil. Thus, it pays schools, literally, to be on the lookout for incidents of bullying and to deal with those incidents accordingly.

As a person with a disability who suffered great torment at school, this law would have helped to make my days more tolerable.

Myth #5: "Judges are running the country with human rights!"

This is false.

The Human Rights Act does not permit our judges to set aside other Acts of Parliament.

In some countries, such as America, judges can 'review' Acts and declare them to be unconstitutional – meaning void. When this occasionally happens, it is not seen as wrong or interfering, but rather, as living proof that judges will defend personal freedom against misuse of power.

In Britain, judges may 'review' those rules and decisions of government ministers which upset peoples' lives and lead to complaints. Naturally, ministers do not like this. Ministers feel that, as judges are not elected, they have no right to question – even though we, the people, have asked them to.

During the past decade, ministers have begun to slate judges through the media. For instance, in 2003, the then Home Secretary, David Blunkett, was quoted as saying: "Frankly, I'm fed up with having to deal with a situation where Parliament debates issues and the judges then overturn them."

In 2011, former Home Secretary, Michael Howard, stated: "In my view, the power of the judges, as opposed to elected politicians, is increasing and ought to be diminished."

Most recently, David Cameron journeyed to Strasbourg to address the judges of the European Court of Human Rights, which is the final court of appeal for any country that is signed-up to Churchill's Convention. Before travelling, Cameron told the British press: "National governments should take primary responsibility for safeguarding citizens' rights." He also said: "The European Court should not be going over national decisions which it does not need to."

Of course, an advocate for human rights would reply that the Court only goes over a 'national decision' in cases where it must – to uphold the rights enshrined in the Convention.

Unfortunately, though, politicians and tabloids are making people believe that, thanks to human rights, Parliament is no longer in command; that unelected judges (here and abroad) are the real decision-makers behind everything.

That is simply not true.

The noble judges are only concerned with protecting the principles of humanity.... as noble ministers should be when making so-called 'national decisions.'

It is worth mentioning a fact here which the tabloids prefer to overlook. The most eminent and respected judge sitting in the European Court of Human Rights is Sir Nicolas Bratza QC, a senior British lawyer. He currently serves as President of the Court. In fact, Sir Nicolas might have become a judge in our very own Supreme Court if he had not chosen to work in Strasbourg.

So, despite what tabloids are printing, not every judge sitting in Strasbourg is a foreigner, supposedly unacquainted with the British way of life.

Myth #6: "Human rights stop terrorists being deported!"

This is false.

It is, however, the hardest myth to dispel because many people do not distinguish between terror suspects (foreign and British), preachers of Islamic extremism (foreign and British) and asylum-seekers (genuine and bogus). For the misinformed among us, these categories all blend into one. And racism, which permeates all levels of society, blinds many eyes to a simple truth: that al-Qaeda is to Muslims what the KKK is to Christians.

It should be pointed out that the four Muslim terrorists involved in the 2005 London bombings were British citizens, born and bred. Had these men been caught, they would have faced imprisonment, not deportation.

In Britain, we do not deport our own citizens, no matter what crime they commit. We stopped this practice in 1868. Therefore, only foreign terrorists can be deported.

But as terrorists are not all foreigners, deportation cannot be the whole solution to the problem. Rather, the trial and imprisonment of terror suspects will help to keep us safe, with deportations where appropriate. Obviously, good policing is needed to achieve this.

However, we can reduce the number of possible *future* terrorists (at home and abroad) by simply upholding the law and not ignoring it when this happens to suit – as Britain and America have both been guilty of. Such hypocrisy serves only to affirm the radical views held against us and encourage more hatred.

The renowned British lawyer, Clive Stafford Smith, has represented more than fifty prisoners held without charge at Guantanamo Bay. He writes: "[...] The first rule in my counter-terrorism handbook is that if you behave with decency, upholding your own standards, there will be fewer people who want to kill you. This is not a matter of 'coddling terrorists' – it is simply a matter of living up to our ideals. It is also common sense."

More than actual terror suspects, the British press tends to focus on preachers of Islamic extremism, or 'jihadist fanatics' as they are sometimes called.

Undoubtedly, the small number of persons who preach these hateful words are acting in violation of the law. They abuse their freedom of speech by encouraging violence among us. And, where such persons are foreign, they should indeed be deported. But difficulty may arise where a deportee claims asylum.

In Britain and across Europe, generally speaking, we will not allow any person to be tortured or killed. In fact, we once delayed an American murder suspect being returned to America to stand trial there. American prosecutors had to give assurances that the death penalty would not be sought against the suspect.

This is what makes Britain a shining example to the world: at our core, we strive for peace. Like all nations, we can appear to forget this at times, yet we are reminded by those brave advocates, in courtrooms and living rooms alike, who are willing to speak-up and defend an unpopular case where bigger principles are at stake. Indeed, we are reminded from time to time that to show compassion is not un-British.

Following the Second World War, at a time when many people talked openly of wanting to grind the German's face in the dust, Winston Churchill stunned the world when he announced: "I'm going to say something that will astonish you." And, setting a brave new tone of reconciliation, he proposed that Germany rejoin the "European family."

Churchill was by no means perfect. He loved the British Empire and certainly relished a battle. Yet, unlike Hitler, Churchill saw the virtue of compassion, and the strength it imparts to all. Without a doubt, he would have granted asylum to any German citizen seeking shelter from the Nazis. And surely, if he were governing in more recent times, no person would have been returned to face Hussein or Gaddafi on Churchill's watch.

Today, it must be expected that some persons facing deportation from this island may try to remain by taking advantage of our kindness. Therefore, it is only right that each claim for asylum be considered on its merits. We do not allow foreigners to stay simply because they have asked, neither should we – and this rule applies equally to foreign terror suspects.

A useful, current example is that of the radical Muslim cleric, Abu Qatada, who claimed asylum on grounds that he would be tortured if returned to his native country of Jordan – where he is wanted for crimes allegedly committed there.

Jordan is known to practise torture, so the claim for asylum is at least credible. However, as of today's date, the British Government has received assurances from Jordan that Qatada will not face torture if returned home, and the European Court of Human Rights has chosen to accept these assurances.

The fight for Qatada's deportation now centres on whether the evidence against him in Jordan was gathered using torture. If so, this would prevent him getting a fair trial, although further assurances are being sought at this time.

Qatada was first arrested in 2002 and has since been unable to preach hatred on our streets or communicate with anyone, yet the tabloids have succeeded in making this extremist the 'poster boy' for the Human Rights Act. Indeed, Qatada's face is used to perpetuate our darkest angers and bleakest fears. What a tragedy for us, and what a triumph for terror.

Terrorism does not aim to defeat us in battle. Its purpose is to make us loathe the very freedom which sets us apart from the foe. They use our freedom against us to meet on British soil and plot our destruction. But the answer is not to surrender our freedom in order to be safe. A people can never be too free for its own good, despite what some politicians may say.

Regrettably, though, a few scheming characters will continue to preach a gospel of blame: that human rights are the cause of Britain's woes; that so-called 'British' rights will make our country safer. It thus bears repeating: rather than accepting things blindly, more British people must try to question what they read.

Be wary of politicians who are using the blame game to keep us divided; angry at one another and ready to sacrifice the rights we have in common, rather than encouraging us to unite; to stand together, despite our differences, in a spirit of common destiny.

Think of Churchill. As Prime Minister, he inherited a national threat far greater from the Nazis than al-Qaeda can ever hope to present.

As Nazi bombs rained hard across London, night after night, Churchill had every opportunity to divert the blame by pointing his finger at the last Prime Minister, Neville Chamberlain, whose timid policy was to appease Hitler until war became inevitable. Yet, in a famed letter of encouragement, Churchill wrote:

"Never give in; never, never, never, except to convictions of honour and good sense. Do not let us speak of darker days. These are not dark days; these are great days; the greatest days our country has ever lived. And we must all thank God that we have been allowed to play a part in making these days memorable."

So don't be persuaded by the grim politics of blame. Look to our honoured past for guidance in living this troubled present. Decide for yourself what makes our Britain great, and don't let a handful of negative, self-interested politicians convince you otherwise.

Success Stories ...

It is unfortunate that amidst the myths, few people get to read the many success stories where human rights have come to the aid of good people facing bad times. For example, the case in which an elderly couple, Gordon and Nora Watts, were forced to live apart, in separate care homes, despite sixty years of marriage.

Many elderly couples had suffered the same fate in the past, but in this case, British social services were not expecting Mr and Mrs Watts to assert their human, legal right to a family life. Hence to say, the decision was revised and the couple were allowed to live together, instead of twenty miles apart.

Stories like this are seldom reported. Instead, the tabloids focus on cases where an illegal immigrant begs not to be deported because he has fathered children in Britain and cannot bear to leave them.

'Lying immigrants.... ABOLISH HUMAN RIGHTS!' cry the headlines.

Yet, many readers fail to realise: if our human, legal right to a family life is abolished, it will be easier to deport illegal immigrants, but life will also get tougher for couples like Mr and Mrs Watts, and British families in general.

Ask yourself how the British tabloids can be so irresponsible, and why?

In another case, a couple with learning disabilities were required by social services to submit to a 'parenting assessment' to ensure they could take proper care of their baby. This is not an unreasonable thing to ask of some disabled parents. However, in this case, a CCTV camera was placed in the couple's bedroom to observe them during the night – even though their baby slept in a separate room.

This was indeed a step too far. With the help of a concerned neighbour, the couple asserted their human, legal right to a private life. The camera was found to invade the couple's privacy and had to be switched-off during the night.

Again, stories like this are rarely printed. Instead, tabloids focus on a wealthy footballer who tried to stop us reading about his secret affair.

'How unsporting.... ABOLISH HUMAN RIGHTS!' cry the headlines.

Yet, many readers fail to realise: if our human, legal right to privacy is abolished, it will be easier to humiliate footballers, but life will become less private for everyone, including you and me.

There are many more success stories for you to discover online. I suggest, let your knowledge of human rights come from the internet, not the gutter press. Then, sooner or later, whilst this law is still around, you too could use it to help someone you love, or perhaps even yourself.

This concludes my introduction.

I will now make the case for *The Judges' Charter of Basic Rights and Freedoms*. In doing so, I am mindful of Voltaire's famous quote: "I may disagree with what you say but will defend your right to say it."

It is in this spirit that I trust my case will be received.

"There are deep problems in our society; a growing sense that individual rights come before anything else."

"This whole health and safety, human rights culture has infected every part of our life. We have got to end this nonsense."

"We're looking at creating our own British Bill of Rights."

– David Cameron, speaking in various tabloids

Petition

This is a petition addressed to all the judges of Britain, but especially the twelve highest judges in our land, The Justices of The Supreme Court:

LORD PHILLIPS, President;

LORD HOPE;
LORD WALKER;
LADY HALE;
LORD MANCE;
LORD KERR;
LORD CLARKE;
LORD DYSON;
LORD WILSON;
LORD SUMPTION;
LORD REED;
LORD CARNWATH.

It is intended that a copy of this petition shall be served upon each Supreme Justice. Also, an effort will be made to distribute this petition to lower courts across the land, where it is hoped that other judges may find it and debate the principles contained, just as in the olden times.

The petition forms part of a book which I have written for the lay reader. A less formal, explanatory tone has thus been adopted to make this work accessible to all, not just those with legal experience. As it happens, I am not a lawyer, although I do possess a law degree.

I appreciate that Your Lordships, and Your Ladyship, are under no obligation to read this petition, let alone make it the basis for any reform. However, as a concerned citizen of our island, I have for some time felt a great longing to compose the document which you hold right now. And throughout my efforts, I have kept faith that these words will not be in vain; that they will find an audience, even briefly, within the sacred space of your chambers.

I wish to point out respectfully that Magna Carta, the Great English Charter of 1215, was presented to King John by laymen (albeit a band of wealthy barons), at a time when our Parliament had yet to be established. So this would not be the first time in history that a petition has reached authority from the ground up, having been conceived by a non-politician at the grassroots level.

Whether or not it deserves the same acclaim as Magna Carta is a decision entirely for you. For my part, I will endeavour to do my best.

As to the legal question of whether I hold a sufficient interest so as to distinguish this petition from the meddlesome rantings of a busybody, I would rely upon the principle contained in the *Rees-Mogg* case – that a public spirited citizen may petition the court on an issue of public importance. Indeed, I would go further than this, relying on the principle contained in the *Greenpeace* case – that if I, a concerned and able citizen, cannot make this necessary plea on behalf of my fellows, who else is likely to?

Thus, without further delay, let me come straight to the point.

The people of Britain need basic rights they can count on.... always.

And the tinkering of politicians with our most basic liberties has to stop.

The time has come for the courts to stand guard over certain, non-negotiable entitlements.

For almost eight centuries, ever since King John was made to sign Magna Carta on a fine afternoon in Surrey, the struggle for personal freedom has endured the tumult of time.

When our people craved democracy, King Charles and his royal army could not stem the tide. Indeed, the King went headless to his grave rather than permit his subjects to vote. And when his son, King James, pined alike for such authority, he too was overthrown.

From 1689 onwards, it was clear to all that Britons will face death rather than live by the diktats of just one man. Democracy, this promise which poor will die for; this force which de-thrones Kings, had been established, once and for all, as the only true way to govern our island.

Eight centuries is a vast space of time. Democracy has stood proud in Britain for the last three of those centuries. But a mere seventy years ago, democracy came under threat when a certain madman tried his utmost to bomb our island into submission, that we may succumb to the gripping pestilence of Nazism. Thank heavens for the British spirit!

Happily, we now live in a time of relative calm, and this is a blessing for today's generation. Regrettably, though, few people realise, and many have forgotten, what our friends and ancestors fought hard to secure.

Today, a single foot placed uninvited can give rise to legal action, yet it was not always the case that "an Englishman's home is his castle."

Today, knowledge is seen as power, yet it was not always the case that an education is universal. And information was not always so free.

Today, just as ever, a false accusation could land any one of us in court, yet it was not always the case that a person is presumed innocent going in.

Today, if a Government Regulation offends the dignity of one's family, that Regulation may be challenged in court and quashed. Yet, up until 1928, the women of our families were not even allowed to vote.

Today, the gay person that each one of us knows is free to enjoy the same legal benefits of married life with his or her partner as those enjoyed by every spouse. Yet, up until 1980, it was a criminal offence for gay couples even to be intimate together, depending which part of Britain they happened to be living in.

And today, I can express my dissent without fearing a knock on the door. Yet, up until 1988, our Government would prosecute people under the Official Secrets Act for writing about harmless issues which were already public knowledge – having been exposed in open court, no less.

The Human Rights Act arrived during the nineties. It gave basic liberties the binding force of law, including many which ought to have been protected automatically, by simple virtue of people living in a democracy.

Therefore, Britain, as a free and democratic nation, can take pride in the progress she has been able to make so far, despite the forces of staunch opposition along the way. Indeed, on this island, although change may be slow to come, we can see democracy at work around us.

It is with a pang of stabbing pain, however, that one should see all this progress in peril once again, as a renewed wave of tyranny creeps silent across our land. This tyranny I speak of is the influence of big business on politicians, especially insofar as tabloid newspapers are concerned.

In Britain, as in all true democracies, we place a premium on the freedom and independence of our press. Unfortunately, the most credible virtue of all, fairness, is seldom exalted to the same high level. Thus, in practice, when it comes to delicate issues such as our rights, each tabloid has the independence to pick a side, and the freedom to print half-truths. And as tabloids account for the vast majority of newspaper sales, this is how most Britons are getting their news – and then forming their views.

Come election time, voters are swayed by their choice of daily propaganda, which is hardly democratic when multiple newspapers are owned by the same individual, whose obvious goal will be to promote whichever manifesto happens to support his business.

This might not be so alarming, except for a revelation that, thanks to the Leveson Inquiry, we now know to be true: newspaper owners are exerting influence on our political leaders, offering publicity in exchange for favourable policies.

This begs the question: who, in fact, is running the country?

My Lords, My Lady, the purpose of this petition is not to usurp the role of Lord Justice Leveson by delving into questions concerning politics and the press. Rather, its aim is to convince you of the need to safeguard certain rights and freedoms that are enjoyed by Britons today.... but not for much longer under present Government plans.

Thus, some of our most basic entitlements ought to be protected by the judges, not politicians.

As officers of the State, guardians of the rule of law, and defenders of personal freedom, you have it within your power to assert the rightful, constitutional role of our courts – once and for all.

My Lords, My Lady, there will never be a finer, more appropriate moment for this to occur than now, when public confidence has sunk to an all-time low due to our political establishment, which drips with the bile of recent corruption.

Politics is indeed broken, or surely we would not have a Government today comprised of two parties whose views could not be more at odds on many key issues – safeguarding our liberties being the most obvious example.

The headlines abound:

'I will rip up Human Rights Act!' vows Cameron.

'Human Rights Act here to stay!' cries Clegg.

And all the while, tabloid propaganda encourages more and more hostility towards the Act, assuring readers that life will be better when it is gone – replaced by a 'British' Bill of Rights, which, according to one tabloid, will "put an end to the interests of killers, rapists and paedophiles coming above those of victims" and stop "criminals using barmy laws to gain perks."

Now, I do not grudge my fellow citizens their wish to see our legal right to a family life abolished, especially when it seems that illegal immigrants can use it to stay in

Britain unfairly. But I have the utmost faith in my fellow citizens that if they knew how this same law helped an elderly married couple to live together in the same care home, not twenty miles apart, then this might persuade them to think twice about scrapping it.

Nor do I grudge my fellow citizens their wish to see our legal right to privacy abolished, especially when it seems that wealthy footballers can use it to keep the sordid details of their love affairs secret. But I have the utmost faith in my fellow citizens that if they knew how this same law protected a learning disabled couple from undue CCTV monitoring by social services, then this might persuade them to think twice about scrapping it.

And nor do I grudge my fellow citizens their wish to see our legal right to a fair trial curbed, especially when it seems that child-murdering villains can use it to put their victim's family through further pain in court. But I have the utmost faith in my fellow citizens that if they knew how this same law would have prevented two innocent men, Derek Bentley and Timothy Evans, being hung unjustly, then this might persuade them to think twice about changing it.

Not for a moment do I believe that the British people are uncaring. On the contrary, I think they care a great deal. But we see this care being manipulated into anger, and the anger then channelled into votes. For better or worse, this is the way our democracy is now working, so we must try to work with it.

Attempting to control what newspapers print is the hallmark of a dictatorship. We certainly do not want that for Britain. Thus, even the most squalid daily rag must be free to print its views, for at the end of the day, the people are not obliged to buy.

However, as history will concur, people living in the grip of a dictatorship can attest to yet another, equally telling sign: the unashamed oppression of whole sections of the community, especially vulnerable persons and minority groups. I say to you now: this is what Britain is facing, and we cannot allow this to happen.

Speaking as a person with a disability, I do not expect that I will be dragged off to a gas chamber once the Human Rights Act is gone. But under its proposed replacement, a 'British' Bill of Rights, there will be less legal protection for the vulnerable and minorities, not the same amount that we have today, and certainly not more. Thus, it is time to take a stand.

I derive my moral empowerment from the sense of solidarity which lies, unspoken, at the margins of our society.

In my daily life, if I hear the word 'nigger' I must respond as though it were 'cripple.' Likewise, if I encourage the ridicule of gays, even by standing silent, then I do not deserve dignity myself. If this makes me a bleeding-heart liberal, so be it. There is enough pain and poverty for the less liberal to console their hearts with.

In the meantime, the real question is not what I can do for my society. Rather, what are *you* going to do for us?

My Lords, My Lady, whether he intends it or not, our Prime Minister's words carry the threat of imminent oppression:

"There are deep problems in our society; a growing sense that individual rights come before anything else.

This whole health and safety, human rights culture has infected every part of our life. We have got to end this nonsense.

I think it's about time we started making sure decisions are made in Parliament rather than in the courts.

We're looking at creating our own British Bill of Rights [...]"

So you see, the writing is on the wall.

Our Prime Minister plans to increase the power of Parliament by restricting the role of the courts. This, of course, presents a dilemma for the people, for when something goes seriously wrong in our lives it is not Parliament we turn to, but the courts – where you, the judges, can hopefully help us.

Knowing that the people have this power is what tends to keep politicians (and thus Parliament) in check; never straying too far from common standards of fairness and decency. But this is about to change, it seems.

Even the suggestion of swapping human rights for 'British' ones says much about the thinking that underlies this reform. One should not require a law degree to work out that 'British' rights are intended for British people.... only.

Without a doubt, if this measure were now put to a public referendum, the unpleasant supporters of a certain 'British' party would come out in force to vote 'yes.'

Now, for the avid reader of tabloid newspapers, I can understand the appeal of having 'British' rights instead of human ones. After all, if you believe the propaganda, then Britain has become a weak island; dictated to by Brussels; over-run by illegal immigrants; always on the brink of destruction at the hands of plotting terrorists. Many even believe that the current economic crisis is the fault of welfare benefits and immigrants who come only to claim them. Hence, for some citizens, it might indeed seem attractive to picture a set of rights which only an Englishman, Welshman or Scot, born and bred, is entitled to claim the full protection of. On some decent level, it might even appeal to a longing for unity; a deeper sense of British patriotism.

Unfortunately, history reveals that wherever a government has enshrined the supremacy of its own race, it has not been long before that race has itself fallen prey to injustice and oppression at the hands of its government – exacted in the name of patriotism, no less. I am sure that I need not provide examples.

My Lords, My Lady, before moving on with my petition, there is just one further issue to cover: the matter of constitutional entrenchment.

It is clear that by declaring a 'British' Bill of Rights (instead of passing a British Rights Act), the Prime Minister is hopeful that this revised statement of our liberty will become embedded within the British system, permanently – or why else would he pursue a legislative format which has not been used since 1689, when British democracy was first established?

In my afterword to the book which accompanies this petition, I argue at length why such a measure is unconstitutional and ought not to be recognised by the courts. For the sake of expediency, though, I will summarise my arguments here:

Firstly, a Bill of Rights enacted by one party, intent on serving its own ends, will offend the supremacy of Parliament by fettering the authority of tomorrow's MPs.

Secondly, such a major reform to our system of democracy should at least be supported by a popular vote, which it isn't. In fact, there is complete division on this issue within the ranks of the coalition partnership –

one party supports reform, the other stands adamantly opposed.

These are hardly the ideal conditions from which one expects to see a Bill of Rights emerging!

The Conservatives cannot have it both ways. They cannot spend one day attacking judges for flouting the wishes of Parliament, then the next day declaring a Bill of Rights that will bind our Parliament forever.... regardless that most MPs do not want it.

I should point out that these arguments would not impede The Supreme Court from declaring its own charter of basic rights and freedoms. This is because:

One, the judges act without political bias and are thus impartial when it comes to our rights.

Two, the judges would not be creating any new rights, nor re-writing any current ones, but simply imprinting certain rights upon the system which exist already, thus putting these rights beyond the reach of politicians – who should not be tinkering with them anyway.

Britain would still be free to declare a Bill of Rights in time (under the correct conditions), but the Court's own charter would serve as a vital 'safety net' which no future reform could disturb. It is to this charter that I now turn.

Introducing The Judges' Charter of Basic Rights and Freedoms.

Or the Judges' Charter, for short.

This 'safety net' of basic entitlements is premised on the idea that wherever British people stand politically, whether liberal, conservative or otherwise, and whatever our views about the issue of human rights, we should at least be able to agree on this one point: we want to keep living in a democracy.

Whatever we might think of each other, if we cannot agree on this one simple point then something is seriously wrong with Britain. Let us assume, therefore, that despite the scandals and corruption of late, the people still want to be governed by democracy – albeit with a cleaner class of politician than recent years have exposed.

And so, if we take democracy as the basis for this petition (not human rights), then what basic rights and freedoms should every person in Britain be able to count on?

I think the best place to begin is with the non-legal, bog-standard, English dictionary. I have thus discovered that the most common definitions of democracy include:

1 – ***Government by the people or their elected representatives.***

2 – ***The principles of social equality and respect for the individual within a community.***

3 – ***A state of society characterised by formal equality of rights and privileges.***

4 – ***Majority rule.***

5 – ***A nation having such a form of government.***

The fifth definition requires no examination. Britain is indeed a nation having democracy as its form of government, therefore, Britain may simply be called 'a democracy.'

The other definitions yield scope for discussion of our inherent, democratic rights. I will address each of these in turn.

It may appear as though I am simply re-stating what our human rights are. What I am actually doing is deducing our 'democratic' rights from all the ones that we now call 'human', for Britain observed democracy long before human rights ever appeared, so we ought to have had a few rights to rely on all along. For me, the question has thus been: what were our rights originally?

There is, of course, a considerable overlap today between human rights and democratic ones. However, if the Human Rights Act were never to be abolished, then the Judges' Charter would exist mostly in theory; a constitutional backup, so to speak, which adds nothing to the freedom we already enjoy. Only one thing would change: where laws are sometimes declared incompatible with the Human Rights Act, but no further action is then taken, instead, under the Judges' Charter, an incompatible law would be declared null and void. But more on that later.

I do believe, unfortunately, that the Human Rights Act is doomed, hence why I am drafting this charter of basic rights and freedoms. In doing so, I have attempted to be economical with it, although, in the final analysis, it would be for the judges to decide the limit to which each of these entitlements should go.

To any who would dismiss this work as mere elementary puff, I would wish to point out the following.

In his book, *The Rule of Law*, the late Lord Bingham endeavoured to reduce this constitutional principle into eight sub-rules which even the lay reader can grasp. Subsequently, whenever he gave a talk on this book, His Lordship would stress how 'obvious' the sub-rules may seem when described at length in a lecture. But he would then go on to say:

"However obvious it seems, some countries do not subscribe to it fully, and some subscribe only in name, if that. Even those who do subscribe find it difficult applying all of the precepts quite all of the time."

This view forms the basis of my own. The eight sub-rules of democracy which I expound may seem to be obvious at first, yet our history is replete with sad tales of occasions when these rules have been flouted or dodged.

Focusing now upon the definitions given, I would decipher democracy as follows.

#1: Government by the people or their elected representatives.

The rights flowing from this first definition are necessary for a democracy to work.

Each person has a vote, and a right to know what they are voting for:

It follows that if people must know what they are voting for, they must be given free access to information. So public records are public property in a democracy, except where true necessity compels secrets. Furthermore, for each person to understand information, all must be taught how to read. So basic, free education is essential for citizens living in a democracy.

Each person can take part in politics:

Meaning, at one extreme, any citizen may attempt to become a politician by standing for election. At the other extreme, citizens may take part in peaceful activities whose aim is to influence the political process – marching in protest, for example. Furthermore, it follows that for the people to play a part in politics, the people must be able to speak out. So free speech is essential for citizens living in a democracy.

#2: The principles of social equality and respect for the individual within a community.

The rights flowing from this second definition protect the tangible things in our lives.

Over one's own body and mind, each person is sovereign:

Which is to say: a person can do whatever they choose, but must stop at the point where they would impede this same freedom in others. It follows that no person's body should be restrained or imprisoned unnecessarily. So free movement is essential for citizens living in a democracy.

The sanctity of the home shall be respected at all times:

It follows that if peoples' homes must be respected, they must be allowed to buy and own property. So a person's home becomes to them as their castle. Furthermore, this presumes the right to some privacy, for if a person's home is their castle, they must be free to close out the whole world. So personal, private space is essential for citizens living in a democracy.

The family unit is inviolable:

Meaning that no family should be separated, except where necessary to do so, and for the benefit of society as a whole. In a democracy, the family unit includes spouse or life partner.

Each person is free to pursue their heart's desire:

Which is to say: the point of good government is simply to secure the general peace and maintain conditions of freedom. The people must then be able to use this freedom however they wish, subject only to respecting the freedom of others. So happiness is the prime objective for citizens living in a democracy.

#3: A state of society characterised by formal equality of rights and privileges.

The rights flowing from this third definition encourage smooth interactions between people.

Each person is equal under the law:

Which is to say: no one is above the law. So the law is king in a democracy. Everyone, from the highest official to the humblest worker, must do what the law tells them without exception. Furthermore, for this right to succeed in practice, there must be courts to turn to, where judges stand as supreme, independent guardians, having the final word on all disputes.

Each person can expect fair treatment:

Meaning that wherever people go, and whatever situation they face, they should be judged by the content of their character and met with standards of common decency. So negative discrimination has no place in a democracy. Nor does any form of degradation.

#4: Majority rule.

Of all the definitions I could find, this one assists my cause the least. I will explain why that is.

'Majority rule' suggests that what the big crowd wants, it gets. This seems fair on first brush. But what if the big crowd wants to deprive a small crowd of its rights? Would this be democratic if a lot of people voted?

My answer is no; democracy is not the same as mob rule.

In a free and fair society, the big crowd gets its way subject to ground rules which are non-negotiable. These ground rules are the eight principles I have enunciated under the other definitions here, which together form the bedrock of civilisation.

Hence, in my view, 'majority rule' is but a partial definition of democracy; there is more to the picture than that.

All these democratic entitlements are laid bare at the end of this petition.

I will now address three pertinent questions regarding the Judges' Charter.

Who will the Judges' Charter protect?

.... Anyone who is affected by state action.

Note the term 'state action' as opposed to 'the State.'

For the avoidance of doubt, any person or organisation providing services of a public character ought to be held accountable under the Judges' Charter.

The private owner of an old people's home should be no less to blame for ill-treatment of residents than the State would be if the home were publicly run. What matters is the service being provided, not the body providing the service.

The courts are best-placed to decide which services should rightly be deemed 'public', but the criteria for deciding ought to be as streamlined as possible.

In these times of big spending cuts, as more and more public services are being contracted out, it is essential for firms to understand that they will be held to the same high standards if they choose to take on the work.

Thus, if a firm cannot stand the heat, it should not accept the contract.

Is there legal precedent for declaring the Judges' Charter?

.... Yes, there is.

In Britain, there is precedent for doing the unprecedented when unprecedented circumstances implore.

One such occasion arose in 1966, when the Court, acting off its own initiative, declared the Practice Statement. As you well know, this was a formal, constitutional declaration that henceforth, the highest court in our land would no longer be bound by its own decisions.

It is apt to quote Lord Gardiner, who delivered this landmark statement on behalf of the Court, which was then based within the House of Lords:

"Their Lordships recognise that too rigid adherence to precedent may lead to injustice in a particular case and also restrict the proper development of the law. They propose, therefore, to modify their present practice and, while treating decisions of this house as normally binding, to depart from a previous decision when it appears right to do so."

The circumstance demanding this reform was a state of constitutional deadlock, whereby it was realised that the common law must be free to adapt to changing social conditions. Society is not static, so neither should justice be.

Their Lordships took this initiative because they knew in their hearts it was right. A shortfall in justice emerged, so the Court changed the way it did business.

My Lords, My Lady, again the time has come for the Court to modify its role. Democracy is failing the people, so it is time to repair our democracy.

The current post-scandal apathy threatens to undo the people's rights, as constitutional inroads will soon be made upon the power of our courts. This must not be allowed to happen. Thus, the law should be developed to resist assault by the executive.

History is on your side.

Declare the Judges' Charter for all.

What if a law should clash with the Judges' Charter?

.... Then the law must be struck down, at least to the extent it is incompatible.

This part of my proposal is likely to be met with the most resistance. Yet, there is no good reason why this should be so.

Every last right prescribed by the Judges' Charter has been gleaned from the dictionary definition of democracy. Hence, if an Act of Parliament were to conflict with these most basic rights, by definition, the Act would be undemocratic.

Of course, Parliament could choose to go further than the Judges' Charter by providing even more freedom and better rights for the individual. But Parliament would never be able to give us less. The Court would make sure of that.

I suggest, Britain has no constitution, but a mere set of unwritten principles which, by and large, have enabled our institutions to get along without crisis. Since 1689, however, as the values of democracy have become further and further ingrained within our system (and elsewhere), so we have seen the friction between Parliament and the courts increase exponentially.

Today, one frequently sees examples of politicians berating judges in the pages of the tabloids. And as judges are expected to rise above such commentary (keeping silent in the face of it), the public can hardly be blamed for believing all the one-sided propaganda – that judges are interfering in government policy and trying to run the country.

It seems, therefore, that judges face a catch-22 scenario. If they refuse to protect an individual from oppressive state action, it is because judges are uncaring towards the people. On the other hand, uphold the rights of an individual against the State, and judges are behaving undemocratically by ignoring the will of Parliament – and thus, the people!

In the *Jackson* case, which tested the validity of the law banning fox hunting, Lord Steyn described parliamentary supremacy as the general principle governing Britain, but not the only principle. His Lordship suggested that supremacy might have to be re-thought if exceptional circumstances were to arise. This view was supported by Your Lordship, Lord Hope, who stated that parliamentary supremacy is no longer, if it ever was, absolute.

In that same case, Your Ladyship, Baroness Hale, stated that the courts will treat with suspicion any attempt to prevent judges having a say over action which affects the rights of the individual.

My Lords, My Lady, despite these strong words, Britain remains the only true democracy on Earth where, on every single issue, Parliament is more supreme than The Supreme Court. In fact, as executive ministers sit in Parliament as well as in Government, it might even be said that, in practice, parliamentary supremacy means executive supremacy.

Our courts thus lie at the bottom of a pecking order, so to speak, rather than on an equal footing with the other two powers – as in countries like America. But is it too late for this imbalance to be corrected?

In a book criticising our unwritten constitution, Thomas Paine wrote: "A long habit of not thinking a thing wrong gives it a superficial appearance of being right, and raises, at first, a formidable outcry in defence of custom."

I have to agree.

If it were impossible for a government to alter its own constitutional arrangements, Britain would still be in the grip of arbitrary rule by kings and queens. Our ancestors took steps to change that, and democracy has flourished ever since. Therefore, if a system of autocrats ruling by divine right can be abolished, why should a system of democracy, which has stood for a much shorter time, be incapable of mere correction?

In his book, Lord Bingham argues, relying on Dicey's theory, that the courts have no inherent power to strike down or disregard an Act of Parliament. On the contrary, I must disagree with His Lordship on this point.

In my own reading of Dicey, I found that he chose to define law as "any rule which will be enforced by the courts." I think this is an interesting (and revealing) choice of words, for if Dicey truly believed that Parliament is supreme in all ways, and beyond all reproach, then why not simply define law as 'any rule made by Parliament?'

I believe that in 1885, seeing how America was governed by reference to a sacred, legal text known as the Constitution, Dicey appreciated that Britain had no similar document to point to as the source of ultimate authority. Therefore, he was careful to acknowledge the role played by unwritten conventions in our system, one of which being that the courts have undertaken to enforce Parliament's rules. Dicey did not want the judges thinking him too complacent about their freely accepted role, hence why he defined law in such subtle terms.

So Dicey defines law as any rule which will be enforced by the courts; not whatever Parliament chooses to decree. I argue that in light of this definition, the strong judicial remarks in the *Jackson* case are vindicated.

The judges may not have created the principle that Parliament is supreme law-maker, but on a careful reading of Dicey, it is reasonable to deduce that Parliament's rules are supreme only because the judges have undertaken not to tread on Parliament's toes, so to speak. Unlike America, we have no written compact which guarantees that the common law shall yield, so this must be taken for a silent understanding between politicians and judges.

I will venture to insert a further, crucial point into this theory.

We know that the common law pre-dates Parliament. The crime of murder, for instance, is not contained in any Act of Parliament, but remains a judge-made law which has survived the centuries. It can be said, therefore, that as judges were once the highest source of law in Britain, having the power to make any rule necessary, their power must have been entrusted to politicians on the understanding it be exercised faithfully – without scandal or corruption.

Is that what we see today, though?

.... No, it most certainly is not.

Within the last four years (less than one parliamentary term ago), we discovered politicians of all parties skimming from the public purse to fund their lavish lifestyles. And, when it seemed this scandal was about to break, our elected representatives colluded together to try and pass a new law that would have removed MPs' expenses from the realm of free information – in effect, making their expenses a state secret. And they almost pulled it off, too.

But that is not all.

We have also witnessed a recent cash-for-honours scandal, whereby individuals who made large, secret loans to the Labour Party were then nominated to join the ranks of the peers. Similarly, in a cash-for-questions scandal, it emerged how Conservative MPs had accepted bribes from a millionaire businessman in return for putting his questions before Parliament.

And still, that is not all.

Today, our Prime Minister, the man fighting tooth-and-nail to replace our Human Rights Act with his own statement of liberty, is embroiled in a scandal over press corruption. Indeed, footage of his cross-examination in court, before a senior judge, can be seen on television and online.

Is it any wonder that public faith in politicians has been reduced to an all-time low?

My Lords, My Lady, something is frightfully wrong when an institution at the heart of such scandal is the same one we must trust with our freedom; when our precious, delicate liberties lie at the mercy of an elite, self-interested few. Surely, the judges of the new democracy could not have had that vision in their minds.

As Lord Steyn rightly put it, parliamentary supremacy is still the general principle governing Britain. However, exceptional circumstances have arisen. And so, I say to you:

Let Parliament be supreme on tax, on health and on defence. Give it the final word on the economy and all such things. But when it comes to our most basic liberties, our family, privacy and home, if someone must be trusted with these, let it be the judges.

Hence, let there be no law which conflicts with any part of the Judges' Charter.

Closing remarks ...

The Prime Minister's words bear repeating once again:

"There are deep problems in our society; a growing sense that individual rights come before anything else."

Now, bearing in mind, as we have seen here, that most dictionaries use the words 'individual' and 'rights' to explain the meaning of democracy, I have to ask: precisely which of these bare minimums does the Prime Minister consider to be problematic?

Does he mean the rights to life, liberty and a fair trial? Or respect for our private and family life? Or is he talking about our freedoms, such as expression, assembly and religion?

If individual rights are coming before anything else today (which I seriously question), perhaps someone should tell the Prime Minister that thousands of Britons had to die to make this so.

Indeed, in 1942, at the height of the Second World War, Winston Churchill made a promise to the world that when the war is won, the "enthronement of human rights" will follow. And within the past decade, Churchill has been voted "the greatest Briton of all time" in a BBC national poll.

However, according to a more recent poll, **62%** of people no longer believe a word politicians say. This result was announced by Peter Kellner, the UK President of YouGov, during his 2012 *Sir David Butler* lecture, in which the expert pollster warned:

"We are drifting towards a political system in which a combination of mendacious journalism and angry voters will undermine representative democracy."

I suggest, whilst belief in politicians is at a low, trust in mendacious journalism remains high – which is a blessing for our Government.

Many tabloid journalists regard the Human Rights Act with contempt, but their contempt is highly convenient because it happens to aid their personal agenda; that is, to see human rights de-throned, so our legal right to privacy will be erased – this having been created, not by Parliament (despite three centuries' opportunity), but by the judges, whose overriding duty has been to interpret all existing laws in the light of the Act.

For my part, speaking in the wake of the recent phone-hacking scandal, I think that increasing individual privacy, even at the expense of press freedom, might not be so terrible after all.

My Lords, My Lady, we see the 21st century ushering in a new political dawn, in which sovereignty of the mob becomes the order of the day. But how long before one referendum rolls back eight centuries of hard-won rights?

Already, the assault on British freedom has begun:

The Communications and Data Bill is before Parliament right now. Once passed, it will serve as a "snooper's charter" allowing the internet usage, e-mails and text messages of every person in Britain to be retained on a vast database – at a minimum cost to the taxpayer of **£1.8 billion**.

This blatant 'big brother' policy is supposedly for combatting terrorism, but how long until people start being investigated for mentioning naughty things in text messages, like watching TV without a licence, or getting away with paying some tax?

Of course, there is no excuse for breaking the law. The guilty should be caught and punished. But, do we really want the kind of society where, in order to catch a few crooks, police and bureaucrats can read through everyone's intimate thoughts? And that is surely what will happen, for at the end of the day, one does not store data in a costly machine unless one plans to make use of that data.

Sooner or later, if allowed to stand, this policy will violate the privacy of our homes. It is inevitable, for when, despite soaring costs, no terrorists are turning up, the public will demand to see evidence of what their hard-earned cash is achieving. At this point, someone will have to be scapegoated, so why not the licence dodgers? Or the tax evaders? Or frustrated individuals who say things like: "Them toffee-nosed Tories want shooting, the lot of them!"

Not that I hold that opinion.

But the warning siren is ringing. The Government can already obtain (in secret) the bank and phone records of any person it wishes to investigate. This snooper's charter is simply the next step in keeping watch on all our lives. And it is also a sign of things to come. So please, allow me to say while it is still sayable:

Declare the Judges' Charter and doom this snooper's charter now! All it takes are your twelve signatures to make our Supreme Court supreme.

On behalf of Britain, I commend this to you....

The Judges' Charter of Basic Rights and Freedoms

By order of The Supreme Court:

Let no law conflict with these most basic democratic entitlements, lest that law be set aside on grounds of incompatibility.

1. Each person has a vote, and a right to know what they are voting for

2. Each person can take part in politics

3. Over one's own body and mind, each person is sovereign

4. The sanctity of the home shall be respected at all times

5. The family unit is inviolable

6. Each person is free to pursue their heart's desire

7. Each person is equal under the law

8. Each person can expect fair treatment

SIGNED:

LORD PHILLIPS   _____

LORD HOPE   _____

LORD WALKER   _____

LADY HALE   _____

LORD MANCE   _____

LORD KERR   _____

LORD CLARKE   _____

LORD DYSON   _____

LORD WILSON   _____

LORD SUMPTION   _____

LORD REED   _____

LORD CARNWATH   _____

"We are fighting in defence of all that is most sacred to man. This is a war to establish, on impregnable rocks, the rights of the individual."

– Winston Churchill, speaking in Parliament on Day 1 of the Second World War

Afterword

Hopefully, reader, you are by now sharing in my belief that British freedom is under threat, and only our politically-independent judges can take the action necessary to save it.

However, for those who are yet to be convinced, I will finish by discussing a current issue: the matter of a Bill of Rights for Britain, as proposed by the Conservative Party.

This document is intended to replace our Human Rights Act.... and *diminish* the culture of freedom in Britain. As an idea put forward by the Conservatives, it is receiving regular press coverage and is gaining favour with the wider public – who, I suggest, are unaware of the true impact which this Bill of Rights will have.

I feel a frank discussion is in order. This discussion should strengthen my case for the Judges' Charter by showing it is a sensible and much-needed precaution at the present time. Thus, reader, I offer you nothing but simple facts, plain arguments and common sense.

Perhaps this is not so much an 'afterword' as it is an 'after-row.' Nonetheless, it is how I wish to close my case, so I'll thank you for hearing me to the end.

The question is: will we be better or worse off when the Human Rights Act is replaced?

Read on and decide.

A 'British' Bill of Rights?

Almost eight centuries in the making, the Human Rights Act had not seen four birthdays when the Conservative Party pledged to abolish it.

David Davis, the then Shadow Home Secretary, stated: "The Human Rights Act has given rise to many spurious rights and has fuelled a compensation culture."

In reply to these accusations, expert lawyers such as Geoffrey Bindman QC protested that only a small number of human rights claims had in fact been brought. But such replies, no matter how accurate, fell upon deaf ears; they lacked the sensation to become the stuff of headlines. Thus began a stream of bad press which, like the profits it turned, would flow unrestrained.

Today, seven years on, the Conservatives are back in power and determined to replace the Human Rights Act with a so-called 'British' Bill of Rights.

The seeds of propaganda, planted by the Conservatives whilst they were out of office, have now ripened into the fruit of a poisonous tree. And worse: certain daily newspapers are making us swallow that bitter fruit.

Now, as I explained at the start of this book: my goal, reader, is not to save the Human Rights Act. I accept that it is probably too late for that. Instead, my goal is to convince our most senior judges to step in and protect certain rights from among those we have today. But this needs to happen whilst the Human Rights Act is still in force. Otherwise, once the Act has been abolished, our most dearly valued, traditional liberties will be watered-down under a 'British' Bill of Rights, and no judge will be able to restore our system back to the way it was.

What I aim to show is that, far from being a good thing, this Bill of Rights is really a Conservative ploy to entrench the supremacy of politicians (especially their own) over people like us.

Unlike the ordinary Acts which get passed by our Parliament, a Bill of Rights is intended to last forever, so it will be too late for us to protest once this permanent change has occurred. Alas, the good people of Britain could be stuck with less legal rights and less personal freedom than we have today. Believe it.

For my part, I am opposed to a 'British' Bill of Rights on three grounds:

(1) it is unnecessary;
(2) it is untrustworthy;
(3) it is unconstitutional.

I will discuss these grounds in turn.

1: A 'British' Bill of Rights is Unnecessary

Human rights, as opposed to 'British' ones, have existed since the creation of mankind. I suggest they can be split into two types: the *natural* and the *necessary*. Both are fundamental and inalienable – in other words, the birthright of all persons, which may only be infringed where absolutely necessary in a free and fair society.

Natural rights are those which we are born with. We can feel these rights in our bones, almost as if they were rooted in our DNA. Thus, when somebody breaches a natural right, it hurts, just as it hurts when a bone is physically broken. Natural rights tell us when we have been wronged. If combined with reason, they help us to avoid wronging other people – because we know how it would feel to be wronged in similar fashion.

Most of us probably recall our first encounter with the school bully; that first time on the playground when another child hits, bites, scratches or pulls our hair. For me, I was five years old when, for no good reason, another boy kicked me in the groin. I remember the pain. I remember crying. Most of all, I remember the feeling of injustice when my teacher dismissed the incident as mere horseplay, allowing the other boy to walk away unpunished. Such is the power of natural rights: even minor violations tend to stick with us.

Now, if mankind did not exist in society, but instead, lived in small family communities (isolated from outsiders), then natural rights would probably be enough to ensure general peace and harmony. Left alone, people would find their own way of getting along.

In reality, though, mankind has chosen to band together; each person living within close proximity to strangers. This choice has its benefits, but it also brings competing interests, so the strong will often try to dominate the weak. Therefore, in order to protect peoples' natural rights, it is vital to create certain 'necessary' ones. This is the flip-side to having natural rights in society.

Imagine a coin. If natural rights were 'heads' on that coin then necessary rights would be 'tails.' Thus, you cannot have one without the other. Examples of necessary rights include the right to a fair trial – to protect our natural right to liberty. Also, the right of each citizen to take part in elections – to protect our natural right to equality.

It can thus be said that, for any Bill of Rights to be valid, it must recognise our natural rights and protect them via certain, necessary ones which cannot be altered, except by a referendum. Even then, some kind of extra 'check' needs to be in place to ensure that referendums are not abused by politicians playing to angry mobs.

This is basic constitutionalism. It is also common sense. If a Bill of Rights can be altered too easily then there is little point in having one.

A true Bill of Rights must be embedded within the system, otherwise it is just a collection of nice principles which officials may, or may not, choose to follow.

I will argue shortly that Parliament does not have the power to embed a Bill of Rights within the British system. For the moment, I ask you to take me at my word. Therefore, assuming today's Parliament can do nothing to bind the Parliament of tomorrow, then at most, a so-called 'British' Bill of Rights would be just another Act of Parliament: a *British Rights Act*, so to speak.

Such a reform is unnecessary because the Human Rights Act already protects all the natural rights of mankind. What possible good can come from changing the word 'human' to 'British?'

If the Conservatives wish to protect us from torture, or 'enhanced interrogation' as President Bush famously called it, then they need to do *nothing*, for the Human Rights Act already protects us from such ill-treatment.

If the Conservatives wish to protect our right to privacy, they need to do *nothing*, for the Human Rights Act is working just fine.

If the Conservatives wish to prevent intrusions upon family or property, they need to do *nothing*, for the Human Rights Act already prohibits such tyranny.

In fact, it is hard to imagine any kind of cruelty or trespass which, if sanctioned by the State, would not violate the Human Rights Act somehow. And, whilst citizens cannot enforce human rights against each other, the Act puts a duty on judges to interpret all law in a way that agrees with human rights. So, whether we are being sued by a neighbour or prosecuted by the State, we can trust the court not to make rulings which violate basic decency.

A leading expert, Professor Klug, has suggested: "[...] In some quarters, support for a Bill of Rights has become code for opposition to universal human rights norms within our law."

I tend to agree, as the strongest advocates for change seem to have one thing in common: a burning desire to replace human rights instead of refine them.

When David Cameron is asked what new rights and freedoms his Bill of Rights will protect, the best answer he gives is the right to trial by jury. Now, to be fair, there have been proposals in recent years to save money by restricting the number of offences which can be tried in front of a jury. It has also been suggested that long, complicated fraud trials might be better suited to an expert judge as opposed to lay persons.

However, the Human Rights Act protects everyone's right to a fair trial. Thus, if the State sought to deny someone their right to a jury (say, where very serious charges are brought) then this would give rise to a challenge under the Act. If the Conservatives are concerned, though, they could pass a new Act of Parliament (say, a *Trial by Jury Act*) to clarify the exact circumstances when a person must be tried by jury. There is no need to scrap the Human Rights Act which covers all the major bases – including life, liberty and a fair trial.

What other 'improvements' have been suggested of late?

Well, Conservative commentators argue that a 'British' Bill of Rights would do better than the Human Rights Act in supporting persons with disabilities. As a person with a disability myself, I would like to respond.

If the Conservatives want to do something to support me and other disabled persons I know, then instead of abolishing our human, legal rights, they can make a simple pledge not to revoke a certain benefit which makes our lives easier.

During the past year, there has been worrying talk of scrapping the Mobility Scheme for persons who find it difficult getting around – including amputees, paraplegics, motor-neurone sufferers and those with Down's. Therefore, my message to the Conservatives is: leave our 'getting-around' benefit alone and focus instead on putting new, even more helpful measures in place. There is no need to abolish the Human Rights Act which empowers the disabled to challenge decisions (possibly *yours*) which impact on our lives.

The Act may not refer to disability directly, but it goes without saying that, in a democracy, disabled persons must enjoy the same rights as everyone else – including family life and freedom from degrading treatment.

A solid foundation exists for Britain's disabled. Thus, rather than tearing it down, the Conservatives should try to build it up. Save the 'British' rhetoric, Cameron. Disabled people are human and we want our human rights.

Other such proposals have been put recently, all equally disingenuous, for rather than thinking about new ways to build upon the Human Rights Act, right-wing politicians are instead finding issues which the Act does not refer to explicitly and using these to justify its destruction.

By way of illustration: how many of us write the exact brand of baked beans that we prefer on our shopping list? Not many, I would guess. Now, when someone uses the list to go shopping for us, should that person refuse to buy baked beans at all, just because the exact brand is not specified? Or, should they rely on common sense to pick the best baked beans available? Or.... should they take the 'nuclear' option and destroy the entire list because it lacks one point? I suppose it depends whether the shopper happens to vote Conservative!

It seems clear, in light of this discussion so far, that a 'British' Bill of Rights is not meant to extend our personal freedom any further, but rather, its purpose must be to rein it in – which brings me to my second ground for opposing this drastic reform.

2: A 'British' Bill of Rights is Untrustworthy

FACT: Under a 'British' Bill of Rights, your legal right to a family life will not be recognised.

FACT: Under a 'British' Bill of Rights, your legal right to privacy will not be recognised.

These facts are taken from media sources. I will address them in turn.

Regarding respect for family life:

At present, we are all entitled to assert this right before a local judge whenever some public authority is interfering in our family somehow. However, David Cameron has revealed that the Government plans to abolish this legal right. How worried should we be, though?

Usually, to abolish a right of this kind, the Government must convince us that the right is alienable, meaning the sort of right that is bestowed like a privilege – and revoked like one, too. So, to the question of how worried we should be, I would say: it really depends on what you think this right should mean for *you* and *your* family.

I will try to help you decide.

The Human Rights Act is modelled after the European Convention on Human Rights which was championed by Winston Churchill. The Convention states that everyone has the right to respect for his or her family life. Without getting too technical, let us take a moment to consider what Churchill and his staff may have meant by these words.

Keep in mind that the Convention was intended to be translated into other languages, so it could not have been easy finding meanings in English which could be expressed identically in French, and eventually in Swedish, Danish, Italian, German, etc. It might be said, therefore, that Churchill's main aim was to get the 'spirit' of the Convention across, not just the words used to write it.

It should also be noted that the European Convention was inspired, in part, by the American Bill of Rights. This is relevant because the American Bill of Rights was originally founded upon English law principles. So nothing written in the Convention is truly foreign to our system.

Hence, the right of everyone to respect for their family life could be taken in two ways. Literally speaking, it could mean that each person is entitled to respect for the way they choose to raise their family (assuming they have one), but nothing more than that.

If this interpretation were correct, the right would hold no meaning for childless couples seeking fertility treatment. Nor would it assist orphans in their quest to find loving parents. Nor would it help gay couples to create a stable home akin to what others enjoy. And nor would it help a foreign relative to come and visit you in Britain.

On the other hand, speaking more broadly, the right to respect for family life can also imply that everyone is entitled to strive for a family using all lawful means at their disposal.

I prefer the latter interpretation, for it seems shallow to say that a person is literally entitled to 'respect' for their family, but nothing more. Surely, Churchill could not have intended the words of this revolutionary document to have such minimal effect.

To use a common illustration: when most of us talk about our love life, are we referring strictly to a relationship that we may be in right now? Or are we referring more broadly to past, present and future relationships all at once? I suggest, people use the term 'love life' in a general way, without necessarily being in a relationship at all. It is a term used loosely to embody our on-going effort in life to find the right partner to be with.

Equally, when reading the European Convention, is it not likely that the phrase *'respect for family life'* goes deeper than the words might first convey? Can 'family life' include distant relatives separated from us by an ocean? And can it include the family unit that we hope to create someday?

My answer is yes.

Like all human rights, I suggest the right to strive for a family is inalienable; that is, it cannot be infringed, except in grave, individual cases where a person poses a threat to national security. In other words, the Government could deny this right to a proven menace like Osama bin Laden, but not to people in general.

Unfortunately, David Cameron does not see it this way. He wants to abolish this legal right in sweeping fashion.

In a recent interview, Cameron said: "If you look at the Human Rights Act and the European Convention on Human Rights, the right to a family life is not an inalienable right, so it can be overridden."

This comment surely puts him at odds with the whole of American society, for the Declaration of Independence, drafted in 1776, begins with the words:

"We hold these truths to be self-evident: that all men are created equal; that they are endowed by their creator with certain, inalienable rights. Among these are life, liberty and the pursuit of happiness."

At its core, the inalienable right to pursue happiness must include the right to strive for a family. Indeed, what more could most Americans pursue in 1776 besides this and a decent home?

Nonetheless, whatever Americans may hold to be true, Cameron dismissed this idea for us. During the interview, he proceeded to cite *terrorism* as the reason for making family life a privilege instead of a right – so "potential terrorists" can be deported easier. He further stated:

"Because it's not an inalienable right, I think we can make real progress on this issue, and we badly need to."

By golly, I should put my freedom of speech to strong use here, for this interview proves what a liar our Prime Minister can be. If his words are true, Britain must be struggling to deport many foreigners whom we know to be connected to terrorism.

What a pile of poppycock!

Cameron was surely referring to one person: a preacher of Islamic extremism, the now infamous Abu Qatada, whose unwanted presence has nothing to do with the right to a family life, but whether or not he will get a fair trial in Jordan, a country known to practise torture.

Even as I type, assurances are being sought from Jordan that Qatada will not be tried using evidence obtained illegally. In fact, the Home Secretary, Theresa May, has flown to Jordan to discuss this with the authorities there. So Qatada's deportation is now looking likely.

Therefore, any logical person must be wondering: why is the Prime Minister using terrorism to scare the British people into giving up their legal right to a family life?

The answer hinges on yet another important right which the Government is seeking to abolish: our legal right to privacy. Before moving on, though, I ask you to recall the case of the elderly couple whom I referred to during the introduction to this book.

After sixty years of marriage, this British couple, Gordon and Nora Watts, were separated into different care homes once they became incapable of looking after one another.

British social services made clear to the couple that they would not be allowed to reside together.... and this decision was not open for debate. However, thanks to the Human Rights Act (and nothing else), Mr and Mrs Watts were able to assert their legal right to a family life and were soon reunited; together once more under the same roof, despite what officials had plainly said to them.

This couple had to fight to keep their family unit together. I would like to see David Cameron explaining to them how their right to a family life "is not an inalienable right."

Sadly, though, there are many similar cases in the past where elderly couples have accepted their fate, doubtless because they felt unable to challenge it the way Mr and Mrs Watts did.

If only people had a proper understanding of human rights, not the twisted, perverted understanding which the tabloids instil, then this type of injustice would not be allowed to thrive. Elderly couples would not be hesitant to assert their legal rights for fear of upsetting bureaucrats.

So please harbour no illusions: this so-called 'British' Bill of Rights will increase the struggles of British families and couples like Gordon and Nora.

It will make life no easier.

Now to the issue of privacy:

Under both the Convention and the Act, the same section which protects the right to a family life (Article 8) also protects the right of everyone to privacy. I suggest, this is what Cameron's scare tactics are really about; he wishes to restrict the power of ordinary citizens to assert their privacy.

If, by relying on terrorism, he can justify abolishing the legal right to a family life, then our legal right to privacy will evaporate with it. These two rights are bound together in law – as inseparable as Mr and Mrs Watts.

So the question becomes: what reason could the Prime Minister have for wishing to take away our legal right to privacy? Rest assured, I shall venture to answer.

First of all, I want you to imagine that you are sitting on a jury. I am presenting a case to you as the prosecutor. We are not in a court of law. Worse, we are in that court which politicians dread the most: the Court of Public Opinion, where far less evidence is needed to convict.

Here is the charge for you to consider.

David Cameron has promised tabloid newspapers (discreetly, no doubt) that he will abolish our human, legal right to privacy in return for lots of good press. Cameron wants to help his party win the next General Election and remain in power. He knows that having the tabloid bosses indebted to him is the surest way to achieve this.

At the last election, the British public were so disgusted with politicians, due to the recent expenses scam, that many people refused to vote. Turnout was low, so no party achieved an overall majority in Parliament. The Conservatives are only in power today because the Liberal Democrats pledged their small support to David Cameron instead of the other man. It could easily have gone the other way. Therefore, Cameron is desperate to get the press on his side; he needs their help and is willing to give them anything, even a change in the law which will allow the tabloids to make more money by printing better gossip.... at the expense of us all.

That is the charge, now here is the evidence.

There can be no doubt that every tabloid newspaper resents the right to privacy and wishes to see it abolished. A short history of the law will support this statement.

Before the Human Rights Act came into force, there was no privacy law in Britain. If someone felt that the press had gone too far in printing a story about them, they could bring an action for breach of confidence – but only if a secret had been betrayed, and only in limited circumstances.

This was not the same as having a right to privacy; the right to confidence was much more restricted. Over a period of years, though, the Human Rights Act enabled judges in this country to interpret the word 'confidence' in a way that gives Britons a legal right to privacy, as enjoyed by people in other European countries. However, tabloid bosses felt (unsurprisingly) that changes to the law should be made by Parliament, not the courts.

Events leading to the change unfolded as follows.

In 2001, celebrities Michael Douglas and Catherine Zeta Zones sued *Hello* magazine for printing pictures of their wedding without permission. The then editor of the *Daily Mirror,* Piers Morgan, remarked on this case, saying: "You always fear that a judge will try and use this sort of case to implement a privacy law through the backdoor." The reason for his worry was clear: only the rich and famous could bring confidence actions against newspapers; ordinary people were powerless to fight these complex and costly battles. Thus, without a legal right to privacy, the tabloids were basically free to print whatever they liked, as long as it turned out to be true.

A breakthrough came in 2004 after supermodel Naomi Campbell sued the *Daily Mirror* for printing intimate details of her therapy for drug addiction. Ms Campbell argued that, whilst the public had a right to know about the fact of her addiction, it had no right to be reading the intimate details of her therapy (which had been leaked to the press). If allowed to print such information, newspapers would deter addicts everywhere from facing up to their problem.

The tabloids held their breath whilst the judges considered this claim.

After much deliberation, the Court finally agreed with Ms Campbell. The view seemed to prevail that not everything which interests the public is in the public interest. The Court ruled that even celebrities who choose to live in the spotlight may be entitled to expect some privacy.

This judgment did not establish a privacy law, but it certainly opened the way. For wealthy tabloid bosses, the writing was on the wall: their days of printing absolutely anything were numbered.

Eventually, after a few more landmark decisions, the courts managed to implement privacy through the 'backdoor' as Piers Morgan had feared. The traditional claim for breach of confidence was extended to cover a person's private information. Courts came to recognise that everyone has a legal right to respect for their private life, and this goes beyond protecting secrets in limited circumstances. Some things are just private, end of story.

Unfortunately, instead of respecting this new legal right, the tabloids resolved to treat it with contempt. This is evident from the recent phone-hacking scandal, in which tabloid reporters were found to have hacked into private phone messages of many people – including the grieving relatives of murdered children.

Remarkably, our Prime Minister is complicit in this scandal to some extent, yet he seems to have dodged any trouble up to now. I will explain how Cameron figures into the scandal, and how this supports the charge against him; that he is, in effect, selling-off our legal right to privacy.

In 2007, the then *News of the World* editor, a man named Andy Coulson, resigns from his job taking "ultimate responsibility" for illegal phone-hackings at the newspaper. One of the reporters working for Coulson is jailed. Crucially, though, Coulson denies having specific, personal knowledge of any illegal activity. Among the victims of hacking revealed in this first round of the scandal are various members of the Royal Family.

Ordinarily, when a person resigns from their job in shame, you might expect them to vanish into obscurity – playing their former position down and preferring to keep a low profile. But not Andy Coulson. Instead, just four months after resigning in professional disgrace, this man finds himself working for David Cameron, Leader of the Opposition, as the MP's adviser and personal speech-writer. And this arrangement continues when Cameron is made Prime Minister. Of all the talented people available, Cameron said that he wanted to give Andy Coulson a "second chance."

It is later discovered that, on tendering his resignation, Coulson received a gift from *News of the World* owner, Rupert Murdoch: a sizeable chunk of shares in Murdoch's company, News Corporation – which also owns *The Sun* and *The Times*, plus a large shareholding in British Sky Broadcasting.

David Cameron cannot be accused of knowing about this compromising financial interest because he was wilfully blind to it; that is, he chose not to have Coulson checked-out in the same manner that every other senior adviser must be checked. You may feel this is strange in light of Coulson's scandalous past.

You might also think it odd that Cameron and his wife became good friends with the Murdochs around this time, meeting them socially on a regular basis. And coincidentally, all of Murdoch's British newspapers then joined in support of Cameron and his party.

Could it be that Andy Coulson took the fall over phone-hacking in return for a large pay-off and a top job in politics, whilst David Cameron agreed to give the disgraced editor a "second chance" in return for the support of Murdoch's newspapers? It certainly appears so. Thus, Rupert Murdoch will have had an interest in seeing Cameron and Coulson reach power together.

What do we know about Murdoch? Well, he uses his stronghold on the British media to influence government policy. According to former Prime Minister, John Major: "[...] He made it clear that he disliked my European policies which he wished me to change. If not, his papers would not support the Conservatives. I made no change in policy and Mr Murdoch's titles did indeed oppose the Conservative Party." The Conservatives then lost the 1997 General Election (by a land-slide) and would not return to power for over a decade.

Fast-forwarding to 2011.

The *News of the World* becomes embroiled in yet another round of scandal. Among the hacking victims revealed this time is the family of murdered schoolgirl,

Milly Dowler, whose voicemails were monitored during her unexplained disappearance.

It emerges that, at the time, the tabloid's intrusion gave the parents hope because they believed their daughter was alive – listening to her phone messages, then deleting them to make room for new ones. Sadly, a team of nosey reporters were accessing Dowler's messages, not the girl herself. Public outrage is such that the newspaper is forced to shut down permanently.

A number of arrests are then made which lead to charges being brought against Rebekah Brooks, another former *News of the World* editor. Investigations reveal that Brooks had maintained regular and intimate contact with David Cameron whilst she was in charge of the disgraced newspaper.

In one text message (sent in 2009, the day before Cameron gave an important speech), she wrote: "I'm so rooting for you tomorrow, not just as a proud friend, but because professionally we are in this together. Speech of your life? Yes he Cam!"

Likewise, when Brooks found herself at the centre of illegal phone-hacking allegations, Cameron texted her a message of support: "Keep your head up" – and, according to Brooks, he signed it: *'lots of love.'*

Andy Coulson is also arrested and charged in the second round of this scandal. He resigns as Cameron's chief of communications – his second resignation over phone-hacking. Shortly afterwards, Cameron stated that he "deeply regrets" his decision to hire Andy Coulson and takes full responsibility for this error of judgment.

Andy Coulson and Rebekah Brooks are currently waiting to stand trial.

You might think it inappropriate for the Prime Minister to be so heavily involved with the stars of this criminal drama. At best, it proves that Cameron is careless in his role as Britain's highest official. At worst, it reveals him in a completely corrupt light. Either way, Cameron's motives for wishing to undo our legal rights must be questioned.

As the second round of hacking shame unfolded, a special commission was established (at Cameron's urging) to investigate replacing the Human Rights Act with a so-called 'British' Bill of Rights. The commission comprised a panel of legal experts.

Supposedly independent of the Government, it transpired that some commissioners were merely intent on representing the Prime Minister's views all along. For instance, Dr Pinto-Duschinsky resigned from the commission in protest because he felt, overall, the commission was "sidelining" Cameron's wishes to increase Parliament's power – by taking power away from the courts.

Ask yourself why an independent commissioner was trying to argue the Prime Minister's corner in what should be a neutral forum.

Similarly, in an interview for BBC Radio 4, commissioner Martin Howe QC was asked about his thoughts on balancing the right to personal privacy against freedom of the press. Echoing the exact sentiments of the Prime Minister, he stated: "[...] The judges have been filling-in the field between these two vague rights without any concrete guidance from Parliament. The thinking would be that, in a Bill of Rights, if the balance is to be adjusted, it would be adjusted towards the protection of free expression rather than privacy."

Ask yourself how this commissioner could come to such a 'media-friendly' conclusion in the midst of the illegal phone-hacking scandal. Do you think the families of murdered children (whose phones were hacked for gossip) would agree that personal privacy requires even less protection than it is getting now? And more freedom given to the press?

Above all, we have the word of the Prime Minister himself.

It seems fitting to quote the philosopher Rousseau, who famously wrote: "The moment chosen is one of the surest ways of telling the work of the law-maker from that of the tyrant."

Despite the phone-hacking scandal erupting all around him, Cameron brazenly announced the desired outcome of the independent commission before it had assembled even once. He told the House of Commons: "[...] A commission will be established imminently because I think it's time decisions are made in Parliament rather than the courts."

It gets worse. At this sore juncture, when Cameron ought to have been advocating anything but greater press freedom (at the expense of personal privacy), instead, he had this announcement to make:

"[...] I think there is a question here about privacy and the way our system works. Judges are using the European Convention on Human Rights to deliver a sort of privacy law without Parliament saying so. What ought to happen is Parliament should decide how much protection we want for individuals, and how much freedom of the press. So I am a little uneasy about what is happening."

Reader, as a jury member sitting in the Court of Public Opinion, having read these facts, I ask you now to consider: is there any doubt that David Cameron is working to abolish our legal right to privacy so that he may endear himself to the media tycoon, Rupert Murdoch, and thus keep the support of his newspapers (and other newspapers besides)? And how likely is it that Cameron hired Andy Coulson believing this man to be untouched by corruption?

Guilty or Not Guilty?

The verdict is yours to decide.

With all this talk of press freedom, it is easy to forget that the right to privacy goes much further than limiting what tabloids are allowed to print about us. I ask you to recall the case of the young couple with learning disabilities whom I referred to during the introduction to this book.

This British couple were made to submit to a 'parenting assessment' to ensure they were capable of looking after their baby. Social services watched their every move on CCTV cameras, as the law allowed. However, a line was definitely crossed when the decision was made to monitor the couple in bed during the night – even though their child slept in a separate room.

With the help of a concerned neighbour, the couple were able to assert their legal right to privacy under the Human Rights Act. Accordingly, the camera in their bedroom had to be switched-off during the night.

But such tales of the 'underdog' rarely make the headlines. They are far less sensational than the sex lives of footballers, or the addictions of supermodels. Yet, if personal privacy is given less legal protection, it is not celebrities who will suffer most, but the weak and vulnerable in society.... and possibly you.

Did you know, at this very moment, local councils and police are trying to obtain powers from Parliament to access your e-mails and text messages at the mere push of a button? There is even talk of them gaining access to social network data – meaning, any day now, you could be living with the knowledge that prying police officers and bureaucrats can read your Facebook page at any time if, for any reason, they want to keep tabs on you or your friends. And this is *with* the Human Rights Act in force! I dread to imagine what will happen when it's gone.

This concludes my second ground of argument: that a 'British' Bill of Rights is untrustworthy.

I suggest, Cameron's plans to make this reform have been tainted by corruption – specifically, his close allegiance to the Murdoch empire, and his curious desire, despite everything, to increase press freedom at the expense of peoples' privacy.

Whatever he might say, the Prime Minister is not fighting this cause for you and me.

That much is certain.

3: A 'British' Bill of Rights is Unconstitutional

In legal-speak, when judges anywhere describe a law as unconstitutional, what they are really saying is: "This law stinks! It offends our whole system. In fact, it should not even be a law."

Thus, the word 'unconstitutional' is convenient shorthand for a host of negative terms, including: flawed, misguided, unfair and illegitimate.

In most democracies of the world, when a high-ranking judge says all that about some legal rule which is upsetting peoples' lives, the rule in question ceases to have legal effect and, happy or not, politicians must accept that they have misapplied their powers and should think again.

This is not how it works in Britain (though you may feel it should). Rather, in Britain, once an Act of Parliament has been passed, it becomes the highest law in the land which nothing can override – nothing at all, except another Act of Parliament. Hence to say, no matter how flawed, misguided, unfair and illegitimate an Act may be, calling it 'unconstitutional' will not convince a judge to strike it down. In Britain, Parliament is more supreme than the Supreme Court.

However, whilst it is true that little can be done to fix a bad law, it is equally true that if enough voters (like you) get behind the idea that a thing *will be* unconstitutional, and if MPs know that we know this, many of them might be discouraged from supporting the measure in the first place – for fear of losing votes, and hence, their jobs. Indeed, it is the old adage that prevention is better than cure.

Without getting too technical, I will explain why a 'British' Bill of Rights is unconstitutional, and thus why your MP should be rejecting this measure instead of supporting it.

The first reason is that it goes against the very principle which MPs claim is sacrosanct in our democracy: the supremacy of our Parliament.

For centuries, politicians have clung fiercely to the notion that, since Britain has no written constitution in place, Parliament's word trumps all. Today, however, a few politicians have suddenly decided that they are free to create a new type of law which will be binding upon every elected Parliament, and every soul in Britain, forever. That's right.... forever, no matter which political party is running the country in future.

This must be the Prime Minister's goal, or why else would he insist on replacing the Human Rights Act with a *Bill of Rights* instead of another, ordinary Act of Parliament? It must be because he plans to go 'one better' than the Human Rights Act. There is no other logical explanation.

Now, as you may recall from the introduction to this book, a Bill of Rights is a very special document which, once declared, becomes permanently embedded within the structure of government. A Bill of Rights can only be altered via a lengthy process which would surely call for the consent of politicians across all parties, plus the people's consent in a public referendum.

On the other hand, an Act of Parliament, such as the Human Rights Act, can be scrapped without having to consult anyone. Indeed, that is what may soon happen.

No wonder the Prime Minister is keen to put his ideas in a Bill of Rights!

But the main problem he faces is that a major reform like this will not 'stick' unless the people, and a majority of their elected representatives, are happy with the idea and willing to stand by it.

That is absolutely *not* the case, and herein lies the second reason why this plan is unconstitutional: because the Government does not have the elected mandate with which to make this reform.

It is true that the Conservative Party has been pledging to abolish the Human Rights Act for years. It is true that the Conservative Party has been pledging to replace the Act with a 'British' Bill of Rights. And it is true that many people will have voted 'Conservative' in the hope of seeing these changes put in place. However, the Conservative Party has not managed to secure a majority of the elected seats in Parliament.

David Cameron is Prime Minister only because the Liberal Democrats agreed to pledge their 57 seats (out of 650) in support of his party. Thus, for Cameron to make this radical change to our system, it must sit well with the manifesto of the Liberal Democrats.

It doesn't.

On the issue of protecting peoples' rights, the Liberal Democrats hold the complete opposite view to Cameron and the Conservatives. In the words of Nick Clegg, the Liberal Democrat Leader and Deputy Prime Minister:

"Human rights are not, as some would have you believe, foreign impositions. These are British rights, drafted by British lawyers, forged in the aftermath of the atrocities of the Second World War – fought for by Winston Churchill. So let me say something really clear about the Human Rights Act. In fact, I'll do it in words of one syllable: it... is... here... to... stay."

Nick Clegg is not opposed to a Bill of Rights *per se*, but he believes it ought to build upon the Human Rights Act rather than replace it.

For what it's worth, I believe Nick Clegg is the sole reason why the Prime Minister has not put his plan into action already. Still, it beggars belief how Clegg, a peoples' champion, could be so foolish as to hand-deliver Britain's top job to David Cameron, then expect him not to do the thing he has vowed to do for years: abolish human rights.

Clegg may have delayed Cameron's plan, but the plan has not been thwarted. Inevitably, with much of the press backing Cameron, public opinion lies largely with him, not the idealistic Deputy. Indeed, Clegg would not last long against the combined wrath of *The Sun, The Times, The Daily Mail, The Daily Telegraph* and *The Daily Express* – not if he wishes to survive with his reputation intact.

Sooner or later, Clegg and his party will be made to tow the Conservative line, just as they did, however reluctantly, on the decision to triple the cost of going to university. When asked *'how could you do this?'* by an upset student, Clegg admitted:

"When you haven't won an election and you're having to compromise with another party, it means that you can't introduce every policy." And he added: "I regret the sheer controversy, anger and frustration, but I'm not going to apologise for helping to create a system which I think, over the years, will be shown to be a much fairer one."

So Clegg can talk tough in both defiance and compromise. I suppose that's politics.

The funny thing is, Clegg's reason for supporting higher fees (despite his manifesto) is precisely the reason why Cameron should not be working to scrap our human rights.... compromise! But, as you are hopefully starting to see, this Prime Minister answers to big business, the press and himself. Nick Clegg is but a thorn in Cameron's side which he knows he must endure for now.

Alas, it is just a matter of time before the Government launches an all-out campaign to introduce a 'British' Bill of Rights.... and hopefully make it stick. But, even with the Liberal Democrats on-board, one pesky task remains: getting the people on-board, too. How might Cameron achieve this when support for his party (and voter interest in general) is low?

The answer: a public referendum. It works in three stages.

Firstly, Cameron watches as the tabloids run daily stories about immigrants taking over Britain, terrorists demanding compensation and couples claiming welfare – all the fault of human rights, of course. Open any tabloid and you will find these types of stories now.

Secondly, Cameron makes speeches to the nation about a need to return to traditional, British values. In Britain, he says, good citizens have no need for all these legal rights; only criminals and welfare scroungers derive any use from them.

Cameron has been making such speeches for years, but you can expect to hear more of his rhetoric as stage three approaches.

At last, with public opinion on his side, Cameron announces that the issue will be put to the public in a direct vote. If more people tick 'yes' to change than 'no' then that's the legitimacy angle covered. Right?

.... Wrong, Prime Minister. Not so fast.

A referendum is a huge event in itself, especially if used for deciding big changes to our system. For this reason, a party wishing to hold a referendum must give the people a chance to vote on it. Either that, or the referendum must be announced at the birth of a new cross-party government, in the wake of negotiations to satisfy pledges that each party has made.

Last year, for instance, a referendum was held on the Alternative Vote. The people said 'no' to change and the matter was settled. But this referendum did not spring-up suddenly. Rather, the Liberal Democrat's manifesto contained a pledge to reform the voting system, and it was agreed that this would be put to a referendum during talks to secure a Liberal-Conservative alliance. Without this referendum on voting reform, there might not have been an alliance between these two parties, and thus, no government to run the country.

So a referendum gains legitimacy either by the public voting on it, or by *necessary agreement* between parties attempting to forge a new government together.

However, neither the Conservative's manifesto nor the published coalition agreement say anything about putting Cameron's Bill of Rights to a direct vote.

The Conservative's manifesto describes what would have happened if this party had won, but nowhere does it promise to give you personally a vote on replacing the Human Rights Act. And neither was a referendum announced at the crucial and proper moment. Hence, as far as theory goes, the moment for a 'British' Bill of Rights has passed – at least until 2015.

Perhaps someone should try telling the Prime Minister, as according to *The Sun*:

'I will rip up Human Rights Act' says PM.

If Cameron had won by a majority then our opinion would be ultimately irrelevant. He could have done all the things in his manifesto, big and small, without asking further permission from the people. An election victory, even if secured by a whisker, would have empowered the

Government to proceed with its plans for reform. But Cameron did not secure a victory; he failed to achieve the majority sought. So instead, he has little choice but to come asking for the next best thing: your personal vote in a referendum. And rest assured, reader, he will ask. He must.

Without gaining some kind of majority support for this Bill of Rights, the next government will have no difficulty erasing it. *'He had no power to do it!'* the new lot will say. By then, however, untold havoc will have been wreaked upon our liberties. Better to prevent the attack now, if possible, than try to fix the damage later.

A referendum should not be employed like a fancy opinion poll; it is a major democratic event. Nor should a referendum be announced in response to inflammatory stories about terrorists, or immigrants, etc, for that is where democracy ends and mob rule begins.

To quote the renowned human rights advocate, Helena Kennedy QC: "If law is completely out of touch with public opinion, it will be held in contempt. But if law were to respond to every tabloid editorial, it would become manipulated by our worst impulses."

So there you have it, reader.

A 'British' Bill of Rights is unconstitutional on two counts:

One, because it will offend the supremacy of Parliament by binding the next MP you choose to vote for.... and the one after that.... and the one after that.

Two, because it will be a major change to our system of democracy which is not even supported by a popular vote.

We are the masters of Parliament. It is not the master of us.

If the harsh tug of reins must be felt, let it be felt within the walls of that building, not the sacred walls of our homes.

If, after reading this, you feel moved to take action, you can.

Write to your MP and tell them not to support the 'British' Bill of Rights in Parliament. You can do this by e-mail if you prefer.

Opposing the 'British' Bill of Rights does not have to mean supporting the Human Rights Act. You can dislike the Human Rights Act, yet choose to wait for a better Act with which to replace it, or a different, more democratic Bill of Rights than the one Cameron is peddling. An issue of this gravity does not have to be resolved on a now-or-never basis. You should not feel that your voting hand is being forced.

It matters not whether you voted for the MP who now represents your area. MPs have no way of knowing who voted for them before. Nor can they tell who will vote for them again. That is why, reader, if your MP receives enough letters against the 'British' Bill of Rights, they are likely to take the matter up with their leader – be it David Cameron, Nick Clegg, or another.

Most importantly, be sure to tell your MP that you will be checking online to find out what they say in Parliament and how they choose to vote on this issue. You mustn't let your MP pay lip service in a letter, only to do the exact opposite when they get to Westminster!

And remember: your vote counts.

To find out how to connect with your MP, see the reference section at the end of this book.

Conclusion ...

At the start of this discussion, I asked you to consider the question: will we be better or worse off when the Human Rights Act is replaced?

Perhaps you never doubted that the Act has to stay. Or perhaps you still believe that the Act has to go. But whatever your thoughts about the Act, I hope, at least, you can see that its proposed replacement, a 'British' Bill of Rights, will be a grim step backwards for British freedom, not the shining way forward.

Still, despite all I have said here, I know there are many people whose faith in the Conservatives will never be shaken; many who believe that Cameron is the Prime Minister so he should be able to do as he likes, even if this means turning Britain into a police state – to combat crime and immigration, no doubt. I fear that, among those who are still willing to go out and vote, this thinking forms the majority view for now.

It is for this reason, reader, that I believe our *judges* should be the ones to safeguard the most basic rights and freedoms enjoyed by us today. And why not?

Surely, Cameron would not stand by and allow the State to separate an elderly married couple after sixty years together. So where is the harm if the judges make certain?

Surely, Cameron would not stand by and allow the State to monitor the sex life of a young couple with learning disabilities. So where is the harm if the judges make certain?

And surely, Cameron would not condone tabloid reporters hacking into the phone of a murdered schoolgirl. So where is the harm if the judges make certain?

I think you get the idea.

By providing this 'safety net' of basic entitlements, the Judges' Charter would make Britain a more democratic place to be. Why should it be less democratic to guarantee, for instance, that all persons are entitled to a minimum level of privacy through the courts? Must Parliament be free to abolish our rights before Britain can be known as democratic?

If the Conservatives are free to declare a permanent Bill of Rights, thus bending the established rules of our democracy, then why shouldn't the judges be free to declare this charter?

In fact, the Judges' Charter could serve to *compliment* a Bill of Rights by providing a solid foundation upon which to build it. For each basic entitlement, the Bill of Rights could aim to provide more, but it would not be allowed to give us less than the minimum protected by the courts.

There is only one possible reason why these two documents should clash: if the Bill of Rights works so as to deprive someone of a bare-minimum entitlement. In that case, the Judges' Charter would have to prevail.

Unfortunately, all the evidence suggests that Cameron intends to downgrade our most basic entitlements from solid legal rights to soft political principles – binding on conscience more than in law. Indeed, this was the situation for fifty years until, finally, the Human Rights Act gave the European Convention its teeth.

The trouble with leaving rights to conscience is that a conscience can be ignored, whereas a court's decision cannot. As history continues to show us: the judge's gavel checks officials harder than the rantings of Jiminy Cricket.

Will life be happier with the Human Rights Act gone?

No, I say. And certainly not the way the Conservatives plan to do things.

Still, one way or another, the people of Britain deserve to know where they stand with regards to their freedom. This constant tinkering with our most basic liberties has to stop. Thus, after eight centuries of toil, the real question is: who, at last, shall be the guardians?

Someone must be trusted.

Let it be the judges.

"Tyrants don't have to wear jackboots. They sometimes wear Armani suits."

– Helena Kennedy QC

Timeline

The following is a history of key events which map the development of rights in Britain. It is intended as a brief summary, not an exhaustive guide.

See, reader, how the Human Rights Act evolved from eight centuries of struggle by those who would reject cruelty and oppression as the way to lead our island. See, too, how the Act came to be condemned, and fast, by greedy newspaper bosses and a few selfish politicians.

As you are about to discover, our basic legal rights did not emerge suddenly; they had to be secured through the ages, through conflict with tyrants – from callous King John to raging Adolf Hitler.

Today, the struggle for our rights continues, but against a new breed of tyrant: the jealous, power-hungry politician, whose success depends, not on winning your vote, but on winning the support of tabloid newspapers – which tell the people *how to vote*.

Indeed, as our democracy is changing around us, so our system must adapt to change with it, or Britain will sink back to her darker days of tyranny, albeit with a softer, subtler guise than before.

My friends, there is no crueler parody than a nation in great chains which boasts of great freedom. Hence, let us take what we can from the lessons of the past, and may our historic struggle for freedom be exalted, not forgotten.

Human Rights: A British Tale

1215

Wishing to spare his royal neck from a mob of angry barons, King John of England agrees to sign a document drafted by the people, which they have chosen to call the Magna Carta.

Parliament does not yet exist. For most purposes, the King's word is law.

However, the people have grown sick of the King being able to dominate their lives and constantly raise taxes, so they make him sign to agree that henceforth, certain liberties shall be respected, and royal decisions shall accord with the same laws which govern the common people.

Over time, little survives of the original Magna Carta, although some of its clauses will manage to become ingrained in the British way of life. For instance, the idea that no one is above the law, not even the King, and no one shall be punished without receiving due process of law.

In practice, these are not 'human' rights, for they tend only to benefit the wealthy and privileged. But the thinking behind this document will lead to democracy in Britain, eventually.

The seed of individual liberty has been planted in British soil, but much more must happen to restrain the cruelty of tyrants upon the British people's lives.

1578

The legal and political mastermind, Edward Coke, begins his career.

Coke starts out as a pro-establishment figure, prosecuting cases on behalf of the Crown – many involving the use of torture to extract confessions. His most famous prosecution will be that of the gunpowder plotters, Guy Fawkes' co-conspirators, who are convicted of planning to blow-up the King. Guy Fawkes himself is tortured, tried and then executed along with his cohorts.

For many of Coke's professional years, there is no hint whatsoever that his legacy will be the cause of common justice. Indeed, as the serving Attorney General, his daily work could not be more at odds with the fight for individual liberty.

But eventually, Coke grows disillusioned with the corrupt establishment surrounding him. He launches a personal crusade to entrench, once and for all, the underlying vision of the Magna Carta: that no one is above the law, not even the King.

Coke quickly falls out of favour with the Crown. He is elected to Parliament where he stands as a proud anti-establishment figure.

Coke soon pronounces a timeless principle: "an Englishman's home is his castle." This simple-yet-radical idea will shape many laws in Britain. And after three centuries, respect for one's home will come to be seen as a fundamental, human right.

Supported by eminent political figures, Coke leads the way as Parliament presents the Crown with a petition for individual liberties, in exchange for which the Crown shall receive regular cash from the people's taxes. The deal is ultimately unworkable; the King quickly disputes whether Coke's petition is in fact binding on him. By then, however, Parliament as an institution has realised its own, legitimate claim to power.

British democracy is on the horizon.

So, too, is a bloody civil war between the armies of King and Parliament.

1689

An English Bill of Rights is drafted after a period of turmoil at the hands of the Crown.

Coming to a head, literally, the days of royal dictatorship are resolved by the decision to execute King Charles the First, followed later by the decision to overthrow his son, King James the Second.

In return for the British throne, the new appointees, William and Mary, agree to sign the English Bill of Rights – which declares Parliament to be supreme.

This document establishes no 'human' rights as such, although it does recognise the value of human dignity to some extent; namely, by providing that no cruel and unusual punishment shall be inflicted on anyone, nor shall any person be punished simply for disagreeing with authority.

But the main purpose of this document is to establish ground rules for future Kings and Queens to obey; namely, that Parliament alone has the power to tax the people, and there shall be no army except for that which Parliament allows.

More than anything, the English Bill of Rights establishes democracy as the true method for governing Britain. At this point in time, though, Parliament is a long way from recognising the full range of democratic rights enjoyed by everyone today. Indeed, it will be more than two centuries before all British citizens are given the right to vote. Most of the rights contained in this document are intended to protect political power from interference by the Crown.

With the English Bill of Rights in place, as cases come before the courts, and lawyers passionately defend their clients, it is the judges (not politicians) who begin to recognise rights and freedoms which individuals living in a democracy must enjoy. Free speech is one example. The right to protest is another. These start out as 'common law' rights; that is, rights invented by the judges.

However, the common law must always yield to the will of Parliament. Hence, Parliament is entitled to pass laws which restrict these traditional, judge-made rights. And, in time, Parliament chooses to do so. For instance, certain free speech is eventually censored, even when harmless or in the public interest. And strict limits are placed on the right to protest, even when protests are made peacefully.

In effect, the common law creates negative liberties, meaning the people are free to do certain things, but Parliament is equally free to limit those things whenever, and however, it chooses. To put it another way: the people can do whatever they like.... as long as they do what they're told.

It thus appears that Parliament has replaced the Crown as the new ruling establishment – albeit with regular elections, at least.

1775

The famous English lawyer, William Garrow, begins his legal career.

Garrow becomes the first lawyer to champion the rights of the accused in court. By his advocacy in more than a thousand cases, he entrenches the principle that a person is innocent until proven guilty.

Garrow also develops a style of questioning witnesses, whereby the jury can clearly grasp the other side of the story – at a time when lawyers are not permitted to address the jury directly. This new approach leads to many reduced sentences and acquittals, where previously, the trial was viewed as a mere formality before hanging, and other harsh punishments, could proceed.

Unsurprisingly, many lawyers learn to copy Garrow's style. His tactics will eventually become the established way of doing things, even in courtrooms across America. Accordingly, the judges devise new rules of evidence and procedure – all aimed at ensuring a fair trial for the accused.

Garrow will finish out his career as a judge. In serving justice from the bench, Judge Garrow exerts less influence on the development of individual rights and is absorbed, at last, by the establishment which he spent years berating.

In time, though, the right to a fair trial will come to be seen as a fundamental, human right. It will prove to be Garrow's lasting legacy. So Garrow, as an inspired young lawyer, can rightly be hailed for making this vision a reality.

1776

America declares itself free of British rule.

The American Declaration of Independence begins with the words: "We hold these truths to be self-evident: that all men are created equal; that they are endowed by their creator with certain, inalienable rights. Among these are life, liberty and the pursuit of happiness."

Some years later, America creates its own Bill of Rights for citizens. Without a doubt, this document is inspired by the English Bill of Rights, as proven by the ban on "cruel and unusual punishments" which is copied directly from the English text. Also, the promise that everyone is entitled to "due process of law" originates from the English Magna Carta.

Many basic entitlements guaranteed by the American Bill of Rights could be described as 'human' rights, but they tend instead to be regarded as 'civil' rights, applying only to persons on American soil. These include the freedoms of speech, worship and assembly, plus the right to a fair trial. If any law conflicts with these basic entitlements, an affected citizen can complain to the Supreme Court which may strike-down the offending law if necessary to preserve freedom.

Unfortunately, it will be quite some time before the African-American slaves can lay claim to this birthright. Be that as it may, the American Bill of Rights (infused with British ideals) will exert an unofficial influence on Britain during the next two centuries.

Thomas Paine, an author who left Britain to join the American revolution, famously writes that "[...] in absolute governments, the king is law, but in America, the law is king." He also writes: "The fate of Charles the First hath only made kings more subtle, not more just" – suggesting that Britain is not so free of tyranny as her politicians would like to think.

Soon, as people everywhere become more enlightened, the idea of 'good government' takes on a new meaning. Absolute rulers will come to be seen, not as brave heroes, but as cruel tyrants; bad for any society over which they have reign.

1832

In response to public pressure and riots, Parliament passes the Representation of the People Act.

This new law creates seats in Parliament for large cities which have arisen, yet are not being represented at elections. The new law also abolishes seats covering small boroughs, where only a small number of people reside. These changes are felt to be long overdue.

It will still be a century before all citizens (including women) are given the right to vote. However, the Representation of the People Act marks a milestone in the struggle of Britons for equality with the political masters who now claim to be their voice.

1939

The Second World War begins when Germany invades Poland.

On the very first day of the conflict, Winston Churchill makes a speech in Parliament, in which he says: "We are fighting in defence of all that is most sacred to man. This is a war to establish, on impregnable rocks, the rights of the individual."

He then goes on to address the temporary suspension of liberties, which has been deemed necessary for maintaining national security:

"[...] In the last few days, the House of Commons has been voting to hand over our most dearly valued, traditional liberties. We are sure these liberties will be in hands which will not abuse them; which will use them for no party interests; which will cherish and guard them. And, we look forward to the day when our liberties and rights will be restored, and we shall share them with the peoples to whom such blessings are unknown."

Churchill will soon become the British Prime Minister.

1940

The famous English author, H.G. Wells, publishes a Penguin Special entitled *The Rights of Man: or what are we fighting for?*

At the time this booklet is published, Wells is already renowned for stories such as *The War of the Worlds* and *The Invisible Man*. However, having grown quite political, he wishes to write about the aims of the war, so people everywhere will know why Britain is fighting Germany.

In Wells' own words:

"[...] This compact booklet tells the story of a manifesto which could be made into a very useful and important document at the present time. The whole world is asking for the war aims, and we British are damping enthusiasm by the failure to make any statement. We are not fighting the Germans. Everyone agrees to that – our Government most of all. We are fighting Hitler and the Nazis. We want to *free* the Germans."

Wells then discusses the rights he believes are of the utmost value to individuals, including security from violence, freedom of worship, the right to access information, and the right to housing and basic nourishment. He also expresses concern at "a vast tangle of emergency legislation" intended to protect Britain from foreigners, which he describes as being "out of all proportion" to the threat actually posed.

The booklet is translated into many languages and dropped behind enemy lines. It will help to inspire the Universal Declaration of Human Rights, championed by America, which is eight years away at this point.

Wells can claim to be a favourite author of the former American President, Theodore Roosevelt, having visited the White House as his distinguished guest of honour, where the two men talked at length about life, politics and science fiction.

Wells can also claim to be the favourite author of Winston Churchill having received a letter from the future Prime Minister in 1902, which stated: "I read everything you write." The men became good friends, and Churchill often paid strong tribute to Wells by quoting his works in political speeches. Most famously, Churchill describes the Nazi threat as a 'gathering storm' – the same words used by Wells to describe a Martian invasion in *The War of the Worlds*.

H.G. Wells will die within six years of seeing his 'manifesto' published. In addition to being a talented storyteller, he was a visionary and intellectual who used the world stage to proclaim his bold ideals.

1942

In an article written for *The Times* newspaper, Winston Churchill makes a promise to the world that when the war is won, "the enthronement of human rights" will follow, and "racial persecution will be ended."

1948

Britain signs the Universal Declaration of Human Rights. Championed by America, this powerful document opens with the words: "All human beings are born free and equal in dignity and rights."

Nobody can deny that Britain has played a strong part in influencing the authors of this Declaration, for many of the rights it expresses were discussed by H.G. Wells in his booklet, which has been debated for years across America.

Also, a special relationship had been forged between Winston Churchill and President Franklin D. Roosevelt, cousin of Theodore Roosevelt. Churchill worked closely with this American leader during the war, and Churchill's friend, H.G. Wells, had been a dear friend to Theodore. It would be odd, therefore, if Churchill's desire to "enthrone human rights" was never discussed with the later President Roosevelt.

The President's wife, Eleanor Roosevelt, will soon become a key figure in the worldwide promotion of the Declaration. She will refer to it fondly as the "Magna Carta of all mankind."

1949

With the rebuilding of Europe underway, Winston Churchill addresses an assembly of European leaders in Strasbourg. During his speech, he touches on the issue of safeguarding rights and freedoms as enshrined in the Universal Declaration.

In Churchill's own words:

"[...] There is the question of human rights. We attach great importance to this. Once the foundation of human rights is agreed, we hope that a European Court might be set up, before which cases of violation of rights in our own nations might be brought to the judgment of the civilised world. Our nations would have subscribed beforehand to the process, and I have no doubt that public opinion in all these countries would press for action in accordance with this freely given decision."

These words mark the beginning of the human rights movement in Europe.

1950

Inspired by the Universal Declaration of Human Rights (which applies to the whole world), and guided by Winston Churchill, a team of lawyers begin writing a 'local' version of the Declaration. The team includes Sir David Maxwell-Fyfe, a Conservative politician and very prominent lawyer.

This new document is named the European Convention on Human Rights. It builds upon the principles enshrined in the worldwide Declaration.

Many countries in Europe are keen to sign-up.

1951

Winston Churchill is re-elected Prime Minister, and Britain becomes the first country to sign the European Convention on Human Rights.

At a glance, Britain agrees to respect the following principles: Life; Liberty; Fair Trials; No Torture; No Degrading Treatment; No Forced Labour; Privacy; Family; Home; Religion; Thought; Expression; Marriage; Freedom to Assemble.

From now on, when the Government offends any of these principles, an aggrieved citizen can appeal to a court in Strasbourg which may order the Government to comply with the Convention.

Realistically, though, getting a case to Strasbourg could take years (and cost a lot of money), so it is expected that, in time, national governments will pass laws at home to turn the Convention principles into solid legal rights. This will allow citizens to complain to their own, national courts, rather than having to go to a foreign court. Strasbourg is intended to be a last resort for citizens, not the first chance they get to plead their Convention rights to a judge.

In the years which follow, further principles are added to the Convention. These include: No Death Penalty; No Prison for Debt; Protection of Property; Right to Education; Equal Marriage Rights; No Discrimination.

1998

Almost five decades after Britain signs the European Convention, the 'next step' is taken by the newly elected Labour Government.

Most of the nice principles contained in the Convention are brought into UK law and turned into binding, legal rights by the Human Rights Act. Other countries had taken this step long before Britain, even though Britain wrote the Convention and was the first country to sign it.

The reason for Britain's delay was to avoid giving ordinary citizens too much power to challenge Government decisions. Other European countries have constitutions in place which already enable citizens to challenge authority. In Britain, however, there is no written constitution, so Parliament and the Government enjoy more power over peoples' lives, and are less accustomed to being brought to book.

This is about to change.

To help the change go smoothly, it is agreed that the Human Rights Act will not come into force for another two years. Hence, around Britain, public authorities start to receive lessons on how to respect the rights of individuals in the day-to-day work that they do.

Unfortunately, the same effort does not go into teaching ordinary people about the Act, and the many ways it can be used to challenge the State if officials overstep their bounds. Therefore, people will come to see the Act as a thing for lawyers instead of a tool belonging to everyone.

Be that as it may, this brave new law is eagerly anticipated – in legal circles, at least.

2000

The Human Rights Act comes into force.

For the first time in Britain, the Government and every public body has a positive, legal duty to respect the rights of individuals in all actions taken. These rights may only be infringed where absolutely necessary in a free and fair society.

This reverses the old situation where Britons could do whatever they liked.... as long as they did what they were told. Now, officials can be summoned to local courts by ordinary people if they fail, without reasonable excuse, to respect the principles enshrined in the Convention.

Many persons in authority are unhappy about this new law – including some MPs.

During this same year, the right to access public records (another human right) will become binding on the State when the Freedom of Information Act is passed. This law will soon help to expose a huge scandal in Parliament, whereby MPs are found to be skimming from the public purse to fund their lavish lifestyles. The scandal, which involves politicians from every major party, will ruin peoples' faith and damage British democracy.

2001

At this point in time, the people of Britain have no legal right to privacy.

Parliament has never seen fit to make a privacy law which applies to everyone. The nearest thing at present is a right to 'confidence' – meaning the right to sue those who betray certain kinds of secrets.

However, the Human Rights Act provides that every person is entitled to respect for private life. This covers more than just secrets. Therefore, when breach of confidence actions come before the courts, the judges cannot ignore what the Human Rights Act is saying; from now on, judges must interpret the law of confidence in light of the Act.

Starting with a case brought by Michael Douglas and Catherine Zeta Jones, tabloids and celebrity magazines find themselves being sued if they 'go too far' in what they choose to make public.

In time, the courts rule that persons living in the spotlight should expect less privacy than ordinary citizens, but ultimately, everyone is entitled to expect *some* privacy, even celebrities. Thus, not everything that interests the public is in the public interest.

Thanks to the Human Rights Act, a legal right to privacy is created for everyone in Britain. This can be raised by anyone, rich or poor, to challenge unreasonable intrusions of any kind.

Gossip writers are unhappy. Their wealthy bosses are unhappy, too.

2002

Winston Churchill is named "the greatest Briton of all time" in a BBC national poll attracting more than a million votes. The award comes at a moment when Churchill's proud legacy, human rights, are enjoying full legal protection in courtrooms across Britain.

Thanks to the Human Rights Act, British people hold more power than ever before to challenge unfair decisions which affect them. Thus, Churchill's promise to "enthrone human rights" has come true at last.

Parliament is no longer the people's master. It has finally become their servant.

2004

With an election looming, the Conservative Party pledges to abolish the Human Rights Act.

Meanwhile, tabloid propaganda is rife. People are being led to believe that criminals can no longer be punished because it breaches their human rights.

Public hostility towards the Act is growing fast

2006

A poll conducted by *The Sun* newspaper shows that thousands of readers wish to see the Human Rights Act scrapped – "to put an end to the interests of killers, rapists and paedophiles coming above those of victims" and to stop "dangerous criminals using barmy laws to gain perks."

The Sun publicly vows "to expose human rights madness wherever we see it."

2010

The Conservative Party returns to power (with support from the Liberal Democrats).

Turnout is low at the General Election because the people are disgusted with MPs in the wake of the recent expenses scandal. Thus, no party achieves a majority and the new Government can only be formed by a cross-party coalition. With just 57 elected seats, the Liberal Democrats are able to act as 'tie-breaker' between the two main rivals.

Prior to the election, politician David Cameron admitted that "politics is broken" in Britain. The result confirms that voter interest is indeed at an all-time low as Cameron assumes the office of Prime Minister.

2011

Addressing the House of Commons, David Cameron announces that a commission will be set up to investigate replacing the Human Rights Act with a 'British' Bill of Rights. He says that decisions should be made in Parliament, not in courts.

Later, in an article written for *The Sunday Express*, Cameron states: "[...] There are deep problems in our society; a growing sense that individual rights come before anything else."

Hence, the Prime Minister wishes to subdue the people by removing power from the courts.

2012

A concerned citizen, Richard Austin, petitions the judges of Britain to declare their very own charter of basic rights, which no politician can tinker with. If adopted by the courts, this charter would continue to ensure British freedom and democracy.

And it would prevent Churchill's legacy being dethroned completely.

References

The following books were consulted in the writing of this work:

The Politics of The Judiciary (5th edition) by J.A.G. Griffith (1997).
I ought to point out that the central thesis of this book conflicts with my own, even though I have quoted from it numerous times in support of my arguments.

Introduction to the Study of the Law of the Constitution by Albert V. Dicey (1885).

The Rule of Law by Tom Bingham (2011).

Decision Points by George W. Bush (2010).

On Liberty by John Stuart Mill (1859).

A Bill of Rights for Britain – a pamphlet by Ronald Dworkin (1990).

Bad Men by Clive Stafford Smith (2008).

Never Give In: The Best of Winston Churchill's Speeches by Winston Churchill (2007).

Common Sense by Thomas Paine (1776).

Parliament: The Great British Democracy Swindle – a pamphlet by Adam Lively (1990).

The Rights of Man: or what are we fighting for? – a booklet by H.G. Wells (1940).

The Social Contract by Jean-Jacques Rousseau (1762).

The Silent State by Heather Brooke (2010).

Just Law by Helena Kennedy (2005).

Sir William Garrow: His Life, Times and Fight for Justice by John Hostettler and Richard Braby (2010).

Other sources were quoted as follows:

"Our judges' backgrounds are completely irrelevant" – was stated by Michael Howard in response to a question following his 2011 lecture: *The Human Rights Act: Bastion of Freedom or Bane of Good Government?*

Foreword:

"PM pledges to replace Labour's law" – The Sun (online), article by Graeme Wilson, 03/10/11.

Introduction:

The 'rape in marriage' case is *R v. R*.

"Britain complicit in torture" – The Guardian (online), article by Ian Cobain, 04/08/11.

Myths about human rights discussed in podcast: "A Fair Trial for the Human Rights Act", by Sadiq Khan MP and Professor Francesca Klug OBE, available on Apple i-Tunes.

The 'deport to America' case is *Soering v. UK*.

"Care home separations may breach human rights" – Daily Telegraph (online), article by Sarah Womack, 04/02/06.

"Council puts CCTV in couple's bedroom" – IndyMedia UK (online), no author named, 24/11/08.

"Time to abolish human rights, says Cameron" – BBC News (online), article by Gavin Hewitt, 10/02/11.

Petition:

"An Englishman's home is his castle" was first pronounced by the legal jurist, Edward Coke, circa 1628.

Former Prime Minister, John Major, admitted at the Leveson Inquiry that Rupert Murdoch threatened to withdraw the support of his newspapers if Major did not alter government policy.

"I will rip up Human Rights Act, vows Cameron" – The Sun (online), article by Graeme Wilson, 03/10/11.

"Human Rights Act is here to stay, warns Clegg" – Daily Mail (online), article by James Chapman, 21/09/11.

"Human rights benefit killers, rapists and paedophiles" – The Sun (online), article by Oliver Harvey and Michael Lea, 03/08/07.

"Individual rights coming before anything else, says Cameron" – Daily Express (online), article by David Cameron MP, 21/08/11.

Churchill's promise to "enthrone human rights" was made in The Times newspaper, 1942.

"Row over snooper's charter" – The Guardian (online), article by Nick Hopkins, 25/06/12.

Afterword:

"Too many spurious rights, says David Davis" – BBC News (online), article by Matthew Tempest, 23/08/04.

"Support for a Bill of Rights has become code for opposing human rights" – was stated by Professor Francesca Klug OBE in podcast: "A Fair Trial for the Human Rights Act", available on Apple i-Tunes.

"Right to family life is not inalienable, says Cameron" – The Telegraph (online), no author named, 04/10/11.

"Theresa May arrives in Jordan" – The Guardian (online), article by Alan Travis, 05/03/12.

"Privacy through the backdoor" – was stated by Piers Morgan in *Celebrities and Privacy*, a 2005 documentary for The Open University, hosted by Mishal Husain.

"Naomi Campbell wins privacy case" – BBC News (online), no author named, 06/05/04.

"I wanted to give Coulson a second chance, says Cameron" – The Guardian (online), no author named, 08/07/11.

"Yes he Cam!" – Daily Mirror (online), article by Jason Beattie and Tom McTague, 15/06/12.

"Bill of Rights Commissioner resigns" – The Guardian (online), article by Conal Urquhart, 11/03/12.

"More press freedom instead of privacy" – was stated by Martin Howe QC on the Law in Action programme for BBC Radio 4.

"Cameron says privacy law should be made by MPs, not judges" – The Guardian (online), article by Owen Bowcott, 21/04/11.

"Row over snooper's charter" – The Guardian (online), article by Nick Hopkins, 25/06/12.

"Human Rights Act is here to stay, warns Clegg" – Daily Mail (online), article by James Chapman, 21/09/11.

Nick Clegg's discussion with students is available to view on YouTube: "Clegg face-to-face with angry students" – BBC News, 2011.

TO CONTACT YOUR MP:

Enter your postcode at: www.WriteToThem.com

This will bring up the name and address of your MP. You can then write by hand, or use the online contact form. It couldn't be simpler!

You can also find out what your MP is up to in Parliament by visiting: www.TheyWorkForYou.com

www.ingramcontent.com/pod-product-compliance
Lightning Source LLC
Chambersburg PA
CBHW020914180526
45163CB00007B/2725